BUILDING
BIRDHOUSES & FEEDERS

Created and designed by the editorial staff of
ORTHO BOOKS

Project Editor
Norman Rae

Project Designer and Writer
Edward A. Baldwin

Technical Writer
Verner W. Clapp

Photographer
Jerry Spagnoli

Illustrator
Ron Hildebrand

Ortho Books

Publisher
Edward A. Evans

Editorial Director
Christine Jordan

Production Director
Ernie S. Tasaki

Managing Editors
Michael D. Smith
Sally W. Smith

System Manager
Linda M. Bouchard

National Sales Manager
J. D. Gillis

*National Accounts Manager—
  Book Trade*
Paul D. Wiedemann

Marketing Specialist
Dennis M. Castle

Distribution Specialist
Barbara F. Steadham

Operations Assistant
Georgiann Wright

Administrative Assistant
Francine Lorentz-Olson

Senior Technical Analyst
J. A. Crozier, Jr., Ph.D.

Chevron Chemical Company
6001 Bollinger Canyon Road, San Ramon, CA 94583

Acknowledgments

Copy Chief
Melinda Levine

Editorial Coordinator
Cass Dempsey

Copyeditor
Toni Murray

Proofreader
Stephen McElroy

Indexer
Elinor Lindheimer

Editorial Assistants
Deborah Bruner
Nancy P. McCune
John Parr

Composition by
Laurie A. Steele

Layout & production by
Studio 165

Illustration Assistants
Anne Marie Hamill
Angela Hildebrand
Jason Hildebrand

Separations by
Creative Color

Lithographed in the USA by
Webcrafters, Inc.

Photographers
With the exception of the following, all
photographs in this book are by Jerry
Spagnoli.
A. Carey/VIREO: 4
R. Cartmell/VIREO: 13
Deborah Cowder: 53
George Harrison: Front cover, 3
Ken Rice: 15, 17
J. R. Woodward/VIREO: 1, 14

Projects painted by
Surface Studio

Location Scout
John Boring

The National Wildlife Federation
wholeheartedly endorses
Building Birdhouses & Feeders.
We have checked the plans and text
and know the book will help readers
attract more birds to their gardens.

Jay D. Hair

Jay Hair
President
National Wildlife Federation

Front cover: Pine siskins are one of the
most common winter visitors at feeders in
northern states.

Page 1: This Eastern Bluebird will readily
adapt to a birdhouse as long as it is not
too close to human habitations.

Page 3: You can get a close-up view of
feeding birds with this Window Coaxing
Feeder (page 84).

Back cover
Top left: Chickadee Condominium
(page 60)

Top right: Country Store Feeder
(page 98)

Bottom left: Two-Story Feeder (page 108)

Bottom right: Bluebird Tree House
(page 44)

BUILDING
BIRDHOUSES & FEEDERS

Attracting Birds 5
Backyard Habitats 6
Feeding Birds 9
Nesting 13

Building Basics 17
Tools and Techniques 18
Materials 24

*Constructing
Birdhouses 27*
House Finch Country Home 28
Flycatcher Chalet 31
Tree Swallow House 34
Robin's Roost 38
Wren Apartment House 40
Bluebird Tree House 44
Screech-Owl Box 46
Woodpecker Homestead 48
Wood Duck Nesting Box 50
Purple Martin Condo 53
Chickadee Condominium 60
American Kestrel Home 63

*Constructing
Bird Feeders 67*
Lighthouse Bird Feeder 68
Hummingbird Feeder 72
Suet Feeder 74
Carousel Bird Feeder 76
Alpine Bird Feeder 80
Window Coaxing Feeder 84
Weather Vane Feeder 88
Country Gazebo Feeder 92
Country Store Feeder 98
Multiseed Feeder 101
Quick-Market Feeder 104
Two-Story Feeder 108

Index 111
Metric Conversion Chart 112

ATTRACTING BIRDS

Bird-watching and woodworking are popular hobbies. This book combines the two hobbies by presenting 12 birdhouse and 12 bird-feeder designs. The designs range from simple to fairly complex. All the building projects are described in clearly written, step-by-step instructions and easy-to-read illustrations. Before starting a building project, however, it is wise to review the fundamentals of creating habitats that will encourage birds to feed and nest in your backyard.

Natural bird habitats combine trees, plants, open space, and sources for food and water. A backyard can parallel natural habitats if these elements are present. By adding birdhouses, feeding stations, nesting materials, and accessible water to your home landscape, the likelihood increases that a variety of birds will be attracted to your backyard.

The highly adaptable American Robin is one of North America's most popular songbirds, lifting everyone's spirits when it arrives in backyards in the early days of spring.

BACKYARD HABITATS

To attract birds a backyard must provide a desirable environment in which birds can live and feed. Food, water, protective cover, and a sheltered place to raise their young are the basic requirements for their survival.

If your backyard provides birds a landscape that is familiar and yet contains variety, they will come to explore and—with luck—choose to stay. With a combination of plants, open space, and buildings, your home landscape can offer many parallels to natural habitat. Plants of varying heights, flower beds, and lawns resemble the edge habitat birds find so appealing in the wild.

Creating Attractive Habitats

By concentrating in one place the resources they need, you stand a good chance of attracting a variety of birds. Also, the scarcer the resources you provide, the more birds you will be able to attract. Offer them something they need and have trouble finding anywhere else. For example, if you live in a dry climate with little summer rainfall, the fastest way to fill your garden with birds is to build a small oasis with water and low shrubs for protection. If you live on the plains, grow trees; if you live in the woods, chop out a clearing.

The habitat you build in your backyard will be part of a larger habitat that consists of your backyard and your neighbors' yards. If no one in your neighborhood is offering water, by all means do so. If most local trees drop their leaves and turn to skeletons each fall, you might plant evergreens. If no one is growing a pyracantha or other bush with berries that will hold through the winter, consider growing one in your garden. The greater the variety of food, water, and shelter in the neighborhood, the more birds will gather for everyone to enjoy.

Plants

Plants are the most important element in any backyard habitat because they offer food, shelter, and nesting sites. Local nurseries and garden centers are excellent sources of plants for your area. Many now tag the plants that attract birds.

If left alone, most plots of ground revert quickly to the native grasses and brush that birds love. If it suits your inclination and neighborhood style, leave a corner of your yard wild to make the birds feel at home.

A yard does not have to be wild, however, to benefit from native plantings. Native plants are an excellent choice for any style of backyard landscaping. Many are as beautiful as those that come from nurseries.

Keep the following in mind when creating an attractive habitat.
• Birds favor areas where different kinds of vegetation come together. Trees, shrubs, flowers, grasses, and vines offer many different advantages to birds.
• Plants that supply shelter but are without edible berries or seeds work only half-time for the birds in your backyard habitat.
• Provide as great a mixture of food as you can. Plant cone-bearing evergreens for finches and crossbills;

A variety of birds will be attracted to a natural and diverse garden such as this one.

A Diverse Backyard Habitat

A yard that combines trees, shrubs, flowers, grasses, and vines with food and water is especially appealing to birds.

plant grasses and grains for seed-eating birds. Offer berries for wax-wings and mockingbirds and acorns and other nuts for Blue Jays and woodpeckers.

• Select plants that will bear food in different seasons. Some trees and shrubs bear fruit in the summer; others bear in the fall. Variety is your guarantee that the birds will find enough resources in your yard to make them stay around. Do not keep plantings too closely cropped—most birds prefer shaggy shrubbery.

Shrubs and evergreens provide much of the middle-height cover in a backyard habitat, so they should be situated close to food sources. Few birds are comfortable feeding in the open for very long; most prefer to have cover nearby in the event that some unexpected danger necessitates quick retreat. Place bird feeders and baths so the birds can reach shrubbery in a moment's flight but not so close that a cat or other predator could pounce from hiding.

Water in the Habitat

Birds need water every day to survive. Much of their water comes from surface sources—streams, ponds, puddles, raindrops on leaves, or dew on the grass—but they also get water from the foods they eat. Birds that live on fat, juicy insects, for example, need to drink less than those that live on seeds, nuts, and grains.

Clean, fresh water is an extremely attractive feature in a backyard habitat. It is far scarcer than food in most environments, and birds often fly several miles to obtain it. Many species of birds that would not otherwise visit a backyard will do so if there is water.

Bathing and Birdbaths

Birds bathe wherever water accumulates. Many will scout a source of water because they are looking for a drink. Once they have found it, they will probably take a bath as well. Bathing is part of intricate grooming behavior that keeps the feathers clean, waterproofed, and in good working condition. Birds spend many hours each day maintaining their feathers, and after bathing most will seek out a perch on which to preen.

The most popular way of offering water to backyard birds is with a birdbath. Ready-made birdbaths are available in a variety of sizes and materials, or you can make one from many common household items.

Birds are attracted to brushy cover near birdbaths because these provide them with perches on which to preen. However, placing birdbaths too close to heavy cover offers deadly opportunities for the family cat—a wet bird is especially vulnerable. If cats prowl your yard, do not place ground-level birdbaths within 15 feet of heavy cover. Raised baths, such as the traditional 3-foot-high pedestal type, are safer and can usually be placed closer to heavy cover. In general, the closer a birdbath is to the ground, the more open space should be around it.

A good solution to the cat problem is to make use of any trees you have in your yard. Set your birdbath in an open spot beneath an overhanging branch. The absence of low cover allows birds ample warning against sneaky cats, and the branches offer inviting perches on which to preen.

Commercial Birdbaths

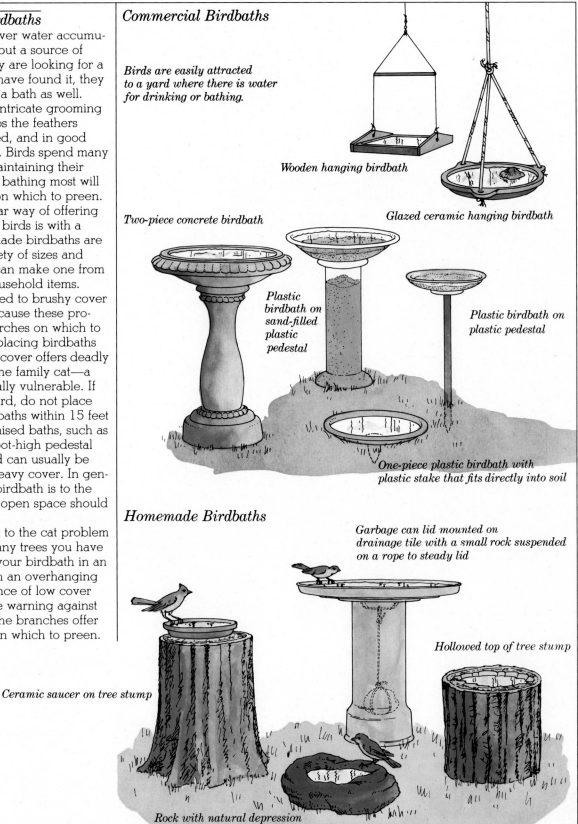

Birds are easily attracted to a yard where there is water for drinking or bathing.

Wooden hanging birdbath

Glazed ceramic hanging birdbath

Two-piece concrete birdbath

Plastic birdbath on sand-filled plastic pedestal

Plastic birdbath on plastic pedestal

One-piece plastic birdbath with plastic stake that fits directly into soil

Homemade Birdbaths

Garbage can lid mounted on drainage tile with a small rock suspended on a rope to steady lid

Hollowed top of tree stump

Ceramic saucer on tree stump

Rock with natural depression

FEEDING BIRDS

For many people, bird feeding is mostly a winter activity, but feeding birds can be a useful and entertaining activity throughout the year. Winter feeding does attract more birds than summer feeding, and for a good reason. In the summertime most garden birds disperse to establish nesting territories.

They do not leave as long as there are young in the nest. Birds that are likely to come to your bird feeder in the summer are those that are nesting nearby. In the winter most garden birds abandon their nesting territories and are more likely to be found in flocks.

Winter Feeding

Winter brings a change in the birds' food supply. In cold climates many insects become dormant during the winter and are unavailable as food. Woodpeckers, nuthatches, and other insect eaters that brave the northern winter feed by prying grubs and hibernating beetles from under tree bark, and they often supplement their intake with seeds, nuts, and berries. Some wintering birds—such as cardinals, grosbeaks, finches, and siskins—are equipped with stout bills for cracking the seeds and nuts that are available during the winter.

Birds that do stay around in cold weather are faced with a special problem. They must eat large quantities of food to keep warm. No longer tied to their breeding territories, most winter birds do a very sensible thing—they cluster in places where nourishment and shelter are plentiful and sit out the bad weather. Turn your yard into such a place.

Birdseed is the mainstay of any winter feeding program. Not only are seeds nutritious and accepted by most wintering birds, they are also

A backyard bordering on a wooded area is a strong attraction because the nearby trees and underbrush provide food and cover for birds.

Food Preferences of Common Backyard Birds

Most birds will eat a variety of seeds, including buckwheat, canary seed, cracked corn (fine), flaxseed, millet (German golden, red proso, and white proso), milo, niger, oats (hulled and whole), peanuts (hearts and kernels), rape seed, safflower seeds, sunflower seeds (black oil, black-striped, and gray-striped types), and wheat. Below are other types of foods and specialty seeds you can feed most common backyard birds.

Food	Blackbird, Red-winged	Bluebirds	Bunting, Indigo	Bunting, Lark	Bunting, Snow	Catbird, Gray	Chat, Yellow-breasted	Chickadees	Cowbird, Brown-headed	Crossbill, Red	Crow, American	Dove, Mourning	Finch, House	Finch, Purple	Goldfinches	Grackles	Grosbeaks	Grosbeak, Black-headed	Grosbeak, Pine	Grosbeak, Rose-breasted	Ground-Doves	Grouse, Ruffed	Jays	Jay, Blue	Jay, Gray	Juncos	Junco, Dark-eyed (Slate-colored)	Kinglet, Ruby-crowned	Lark, Horned	Longspur, Lapland	Martin, Purple	Meadowlarks	Mockingbirds	Nuthatch, Red-breasted	Nuthatch, White-breasted	Orioles	Oriole, Hooded	Oriole, Northern (Baltimore)	Oriole, Scott's	Pheasants
Apples (baked)		•																																						
Apples (raw)						•							•											•									•				•			
Bananas			•			•	•						•																•				•							
Bayberries								•																																
Biscuits (baking powder)		•																																						
Biscuits (dog)					•		•				•													•					•					•	•			•		
Chaff (barn floor sweepings)					•																													•	•					
Cheese (cottage or pot)	•					•																																		
Cherries (canned or fresh)						•																																		
Corn bread											•																													
Crabapples (frozen)														•																										
Cranberries (canned or fresh)						•													•																					
Crumbs (cake, cracker, & cookie)						•																		•		•														
Grape jelly																																								•
Grapes		•											•					•						•									•					•	•	•
Oats (rolled)																												•												
Oranges						•														•													•						•	
Pecan meats (broken or ground)	•	•	•			•		•	•				•	•									•			•			•		•									
Pie crust (dry)		•				•	•				•																		•										•	
Potatoes (fried or baked)						•						•														•														
Poultry eggshells (crushed)																										•						•								
Rice												•																												
Seeds Barrel cactus seeds*				•									•																											
Cantaloupe seeds																																					•	•		
Pumpkin seeds (ground)							•																						•								•			
Squash seeds (broken)							•																						•								•			
Soybeans													•									•										•								•
Strawberries		•				•																											•							
Tomatoes (fresh)						•																																		
Watermelon (pulp or rind)												•				•																	•					•		

Adapted from "Food List for Birds" from *Songbirds in Your Garden* by John K. Terres (Thomas Y. Crowell) © 1953, © 1968 by John K. Terres. Reprinted by permission of Harper & Row, Publishers, Inc.

* In Southwest

Food Preferences of Common Backyard Birds

Food	Pigeon, Band-tailed	Pyrrhuloxia	Robin, American	Quails	Quail, Bobwhite	Sapsucker, Yellow-bellied	Siskin, Pine	Sparrow, American Tree	Sparrow, Black-throated	Sparrow, Chipping	Sparrow, Field	Sparrow, House	Sparrow, White-crowned	Starlings	Tanagers	Tanager, Scarlet	Tanager, Summer	Tanager, Western	Thrasher, Brown	Thrasher, California	Thrasher, Curve-billed	Thrushes	Thrush, Hermit	Thrush, Swainson's	Titmouse, Tufted	Towhees	Towhee, Green-tailed	Warblers	Warbler, Orange-crowned	Warbler, Tennessee	Warbler, Yellow-rumped (Myrtle)	Waxwing, Cedar	Woodpeckers	Woodpecker, Acorn	Woodpecker, Hairy	Woodpecker, Red-bellied	Wren, Cactus	Wren, Carolina	Wren, House
Apples (baked)			•																																				
Apples (raw)			•										•			•		•								•					•					•	•	•	
Bananas																•		•											•							•		•	
Bayberries																																•							
Biscuits (baking powder)			•																																				
Biscuits (dog)								•					•																										
Chaff (barn floor sweepings)				•				•																															
Cheese (cottage or pot)			•																																			•	
Cherries (canned or fresh)			•													•	•				•											•							
Corn bread																																							
Crabapples (frozen)			•																													•							
Cranberries (canned or fresh)			•										•																										
Crumbs (cake, cracker, & cookie)										•	•														•														
Grape jelly						•																										•							
Grapes			•													•		•					•			•	•					•		•					
Oats (rolled)	•			•														•																					
Oranges															•	•	•	•														•				•			
Pecan meats (broken or ground)			•			•				•			•											•	•									•				•	•
Pie crust (dry)															•		•	•							•														•
Potatoes (fried or baked)														•						•																•			
Poultry eggshells (crushed)																																							
Rice					•								•																										
Seeds Barrel cactus seeds*									•				•														•												
Cantaloupe seeds												•																											
Pumpkin seeds (ground)						•																										•							
Squash seeds (broken)																																							
Soybeans				•																																			
Strawberries				•	•																																		
Tomatoes (fresh)		•											•																•										
Watermelon (pulp or rind)																													•										

* In Southwest

inexpensive, easily stored, and convenient to use.

Several nonmigratory species come to depend on food you offer during the winter, and if you are the only person in your neighborhood that feeds birds, it is a good idea to keep feeding them until spring has come to stay. This is especially true during bad weather when birds might not locate a new source of food quickly enough to stay alive.

Summer Feeding

The North American summer is rich in insects, seeds, fruits, berries, worms, nectar, and many other bird delicacies. This is, after all, why the birds come here to nest in the first place. Birds with young to feed seek out the richest food sources they can find. The only birds likely to come to a summer feeder are those that happen to be nesting nearby. A bird feeder may convince a winter resident to nest nearby rather than take its chances somewhere else.

Summer birds will consume all the foods you offered through the winter, but do not expect your seed to disappear as quickly in July as it did in December; now you are feeding pairs of birds, not flocks.

Placing Feeders

Feeders attract greater numbers and varieties of birds if they are placed at logical locations around your backyard. Experiment with different spots before choosing one. Birds like their food sources to be predictable so, once you find locations that seem to work, stick with them through the winter. Here are some suggestions for placing feeders around your yard.
• Set out as many feeders as you have the inclination and space for. You may want to group three or four feeders together in stations scattered around the yard. If your yard is large enough, space the stations about 50 feet apart. Put different types of seed or mixtures of seed in each feeder and include a suet feeder or two for

insect-eating birds. Multiple feeding stations make it difficult for aggressive birds to dominate all the feeders in the yard at once.
• Many birds like to dart quickly to a feeder, grab a few seeds, and return to the safety of a tree or bush, so place feeders within an easy flight to cover and perches. Birds feeding out in the open are particularly vulnerable to hawks, shrikes, and other avian predators.
• Place feeders in sheltered spots where they are not exposed to the full force of winter winds. Suspended feeders swaying in high winds discourage birds and scatter seed.

Because cold winds rapidly rob small birds of their warmth, the south side of a house is usually the best place for feeders. Large tree trunks and heavy shrubs also provide a sheltered feeding site.
• Place feeders at varying distances from the house. This attracts most of the birds to where you can see them and provides the shyer species with a place to feed.
• Sparrows, doves, and other ground feeders usually eat small seeds. If you are offering mixed seed in your feeders, you may find that these birds have plenty to eat just by cleaning up what other birds spill.

Protecting Backyard Feeders

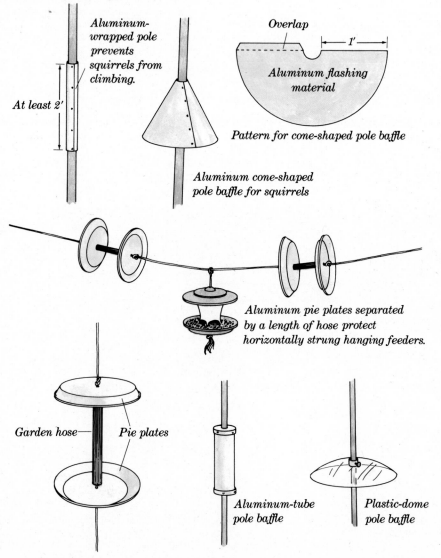

Aluminum-wrapped pole prevents squirrels from climbing.

At least 2'

Overlap

1'

Aluminum flashing material

Pattern for cone-shaped pole baffle

Aluminum cone-shaped pole baffle for squirrels

Aluminum pie plates separated by a length of hose protect horizontally strung hanging feeders.

Garden hose   Pie plates

Aluminum-tube pole baffle

Plastic-dome pole baffle

NESTING

Nests are temporary quarters built for the single purpose of protecting eggs and young birds and can be anything from a simple pile of sticks to an intricately woven feat of engineering. Most common garden birds hatch naked, helpless young, and their nests are often carefully constructed and cleverly hidden.

Most songbirds place their cuplike nests firmly in the upright crotch of a tree or shrub or at the fork in a branch. They start with a framework of twigs and add layers of other materials including grass, leaves, the down of plants, strips of bark, spiderwebs, moss, feathers, and animal hair.

A wide array of common household products are similar to nesting material and are readily accepted by birds. Birds eagerly accept almost any material that is soft and can be easily woven: string, yarn, and bits of cloth. Any household material that may end up being used to build a nest should be clean and dry.

Birdhouses

It is an unusual backyard that has a selection of natural cavities for nesting birds. The backyard birder must supply artificial cavities. The easiest way to do this is with a birdhouse—a simple structure with four walls, a roof, a floor, and a hole for the bird to enter and exit. The best time to erect a birdhouse is in autumn. During the winter it will season and become more attractive to birds as it weathers. In addition, putting up the birdhouse before the trees are bare lets you see how much sun or shade it will have through the nesting season. If necessary, you can adjust the position before nesting birds arrive (see "Placing the Birdhouse," on page 15, to learn about the conditions birds prefer).

The exterior look of a birdhouse may mean something to you and how it fits with your garden decor, but it will mean nothing to birds. It is the inside that interests them, and the inside is, after all, only a cavity.

To offer a birdhouse that birds will use, consider the following.
• The most critical dimension of any birdhouse is the diameter of the entrance hole.
• The area below the entrance hole inside the house should be a bit rough so that birds can get a grip when climbing out.
• Include ventilation holes in the top of the walls.

Bluebirds are among the many species that seek out cavities in trees in which to build their nests.

• The roof of a birdhouse should extend well over the front and sides to keep water away from the entrance and ventilation holes.

• Be sure the roof fits snugly over the entire box so that water will not seep in. A mounting board should be screwed or nailed to a completed birdhouse in such a way that it does not prevent the roof from fitting tightly over all four sides.

• One piece of any birdhouse should be hinged in some way to allow for cleaning. Hinging the front or one of the sides allows the most complete access, but a removable roof or floor also works.

• With the exception of wrens, birds do not tolerate swaying birdhouses. Birdhouses should be firmly anchored to a post, a tree, or the side of a building.

Materials to Offer Nesting Birds

Bits of fur
Bristles from an old paint brush
Cotton
Dental floss
Dried grass
Dried sphagnum moss
Excelsior (wood shavings)
Feathers
Hair (cleaned from hairbrush)
Horsehair
Kapok
Knitting yarn
Pieces of soft cloth
Raveled burlap
Raveled rope
Spanish moss
String
Stuffing from old furniture
Thread
Wool

Adapted from *The New Handbook of Attracting Birds,* Second Edition, by Thomas P. McElroy, Jr. (New York: Alfred A. Knopf). Copyright© 1960 by Alfred A. Knopf, Inc.

This Northern Flicker brings food to its chick nested in the cavity of a tree.

Building With Wood

The best material for building birdhouses is wood; no other substance insulates and protects birds better. Because it is easy to work with and readily obtained, wood has advantages for the home hobbyist, too. By far the best kinds of wood for birdhouses are redwood and cedar, which are high in natural resins and stand up against the weather for many years. Pine, fir, and other soft woods are widely available and tend to be less expensive than the best woods. It is not necessary to use top-grade lumber, but the wood should always be thoroughly dry before it is worked.

When you choose lumber for a birdhouse, give it a sniff test. If you detect an odor of creosote or other chemicals, or if the wood is the least bit sticky, it is unsuitable for birds. Do not treat the inside surface of a birdhouse with chemicals of any kind. Never use green, copper-based wood preservatives, or lumber that has been treated with them, because they are toxic.

Placing the Birdhouse

An unoccupied birdhouse is usually an indication that it has been placed in the wrong location. Consider the kind of nesting conditions the birdhouse is meant to duplicate: Natural nesting cavities are often in dead trees and branches that are in bright sun. Most birdhouses end up in just the opposite kinds of locations, tucked among the lush branches of big trees. Some birds like heavily shaded houses, but many would rather be in sunny areas. It is impossible to know precisely which birds you may attract to your birdhouse. However, if you can provide an attractive habitat, you should welcome whatever species chooses to raise a family in your birdhouse.

Nesting birds are territorial, and instinct determines their location and density in a landscape. Some birds nest much closer together than others. Territoriality between different species of birds is not nearly as strong as that between two individuals of the same species. Even so, only a few species will nest right next to a different one. For best results, spread your birdhouses throughout your yard as much as conditions permit.

Cleaning the Birdhouse

Like other animals, birds can host an assortment of lice, mites, and other pests. Although these pests pose no danger to humans, their effects range from making life uncomfortable for the birds to causing significant nestling mortality.

Many birds discourage parasites by refusing to use the same nest twice. But even if birds are willing to reuse old nests, do not let them do it. Watch your birdhouses. Each time a brood is fledged, open up the house, sweep out the old nest, and wash the house with water. If you see evidence of lice or mites, dust the interior with a specially prepared bird miticide that can be purchased from a pet store. Leave the birdhouse open until it is thoroughly dry, then close it up so the birds can get started on their next brood.

After the last brood in the fall, clean out birdhouses as described in the preceding paragraph and discourage mice or squirrels from nesting in them by sealing the entrance holes. This also prevents starlings and House Sparrows from taking early possession of the house in the spring. Slip plastic bags over the tops of the houses to keep out the worst of the winter weather, or take them from their mounts and store them indoors. Be sure to put them back up, clean and ready for birds, by late February or early March.

Many people leave their birdhouses open through the winter to provide shelter for cold-weather birds. Some winter birds that are cavity nesters in summer—and a few that are not—crowd into birdhouses on cold nights. The houses provide shelter from the wind and capture the heat given off by the birds' bodies. If birdhouses are left open through the winter, make sure you clean them out in February to prepare for the spring arrival of nesting birds.

A birdhouse should be cleaned with a brush and garden hose after each brood of chicks has left the nest.

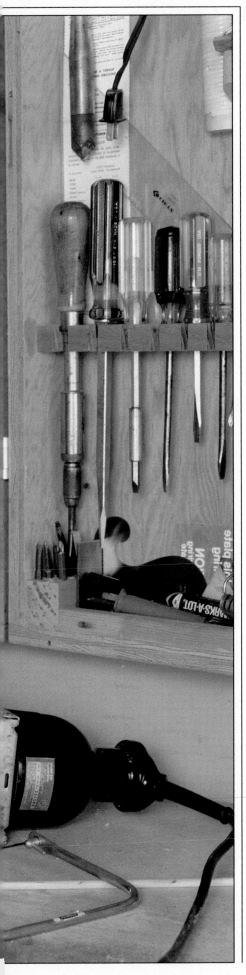

BUILDING BASICS

This book assumes a basic knowledge of woodworking and some of the more common power tools, especially the portable ones. More experienced woodworkers will find several projects in this book that are complex enough to challenge their skills and interests. Novices will find enough simpler projects to experience great satisfaction upon their successful completion. This chapter describes the particular tools and materials to use and the techniques that, applied to the building of birdhouses and bird feeders, should make the job more enjoyable for either experienced or beginning woodworkers.

A workshop that is well equipped with the right kinds of tools will help make the building of the birdhouses or bird feeders in this book proceed smoothly.

TOOLS AND TECHNIQUES

W hether a novice or an experienced woodworker, review this section to make sure you use the right tools and techniques in building your birdhouse or bird feeder.

Power Tools

Electrically powered tools make even simple projects, such as the ones in this book, immeasurably easier and provide more satisfactory results than hand tools. Power tools are widely available at home improvement centers, hardware stores, and many discount stores. Such tools include drills, drill press stands, sanders, jigsaws,

Table Saw

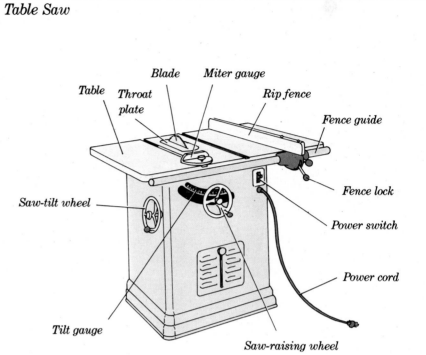

Blade
Miter gauge
Table
Throat plate
Rip fence
Fence guide
Saw-tilt wheel
Fence lock
Power switch
Power cord
Tilt gauge
Saw-raising wheel

Radial Arm Saw

Types of Radial Arm Saw Blades

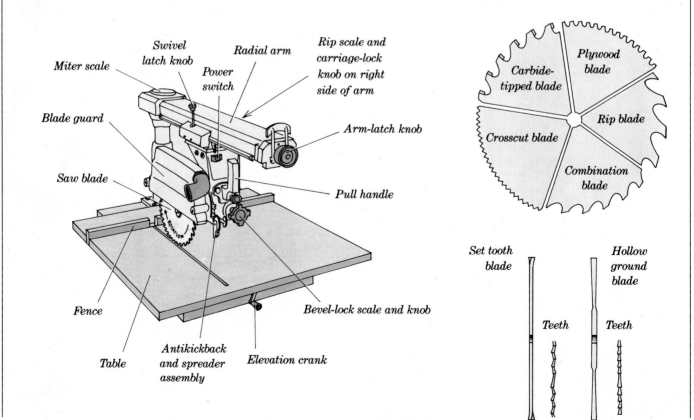

Swivel latch knob
Radial arm
Rip scale and carriage-lock knob on right side of arm
Miter scale
Power switch
Blade guard
Arm-latch knob
Saw blade
Pull handle
Fence
Bevel-lock scale and knob
Table
Antikickback and spreader assembly
Elevation crank

Carbide-tipped blade
Plywood blade
Rip blade
Crosscut blade
Combination blade

Set tooth blade
Hollow ground blade
Teeth
Teeth

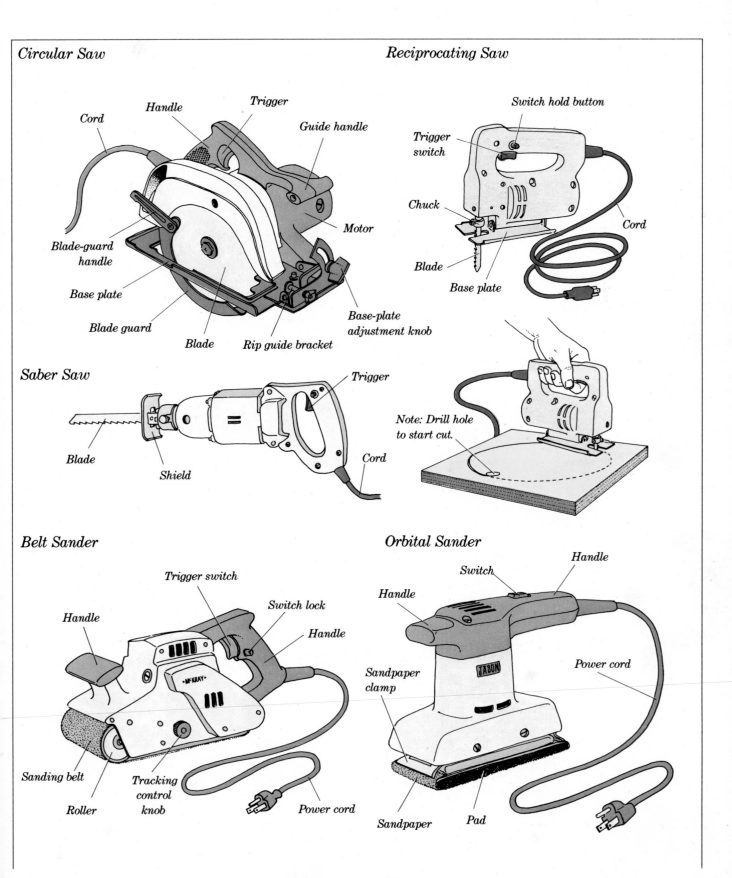

Circular Saw

Cord

Handle

Trigger

Guide handle

Blade-guard handle

Motor

Base plate

Blade guard

Blade

Rip guide bracket

Base-plate adjustment knob

Reciprocating Saw

Switch hold button

Trigger switch

Chuck

Blade

Base plate

Cord

Saber Saw

Blade

Shield

Trigger

Cord

Note: Drill hole to start cut.

Belt Sander

Trigger switch

Switch lock

Handle

Handle

Sanding belt

Roller

Tracking control knob

Power cord

Orbital Sander

Switch

Handle

Handle

Sandpaper clamp

Power cord

Sandpaper

Pad

Handsaws

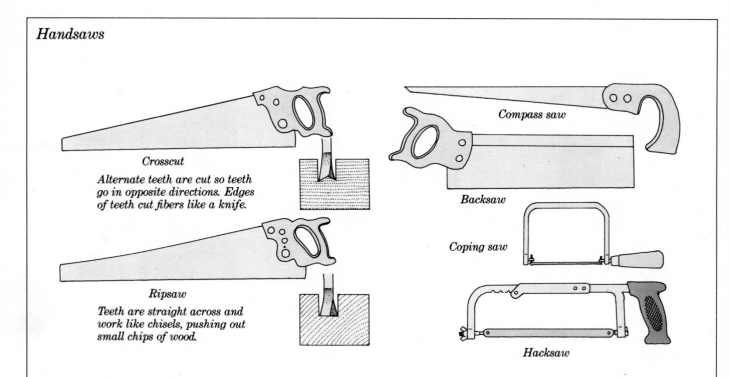

Crosscut
Alternate teeth are cut so teeth go in opposite directions. Edges of teeth cut fibers like a knife.

Ripsaw
Teeth are straight across and work like chisels, pushing out small chips of wood.

Compass saw

Backsaw

Coping saw

Hacksaw

and the like. Many home workshop varieties cost only $15 to $40 and are reasonably safe to use. Many small bench-top stationary tools for home use—such as table saws, scroll saws, and drill presses—can be acquired for around $100. Even if you don't own all the required power tools, they are often available from a friend, a school woodworking shop, or a public hobby center.

Clamps and Vises

Some of the projects require clamping. You should have one or two 4- or 5-inch C-clamps and at least two small bar clamps.

Clamps can leave ugly mars, especially in softwoods such as cedar, redwood, and pine. To prevent mars, use pads made from scraps of thin wood or other smooth material. Use waxed paper between the clamped piece and the pad. This will prevent sticking, should glue find its way onto the pad.

The jaws of woodworking vises are smooth to prevent damage to the wood. However, the do-it-yourselfer may have only a vise for metalwork. In that case, use the same precautions used with clamps—that is, use pads between the vise jaws and the wood to prevent marring.

Kinds of Cuts

When building a birdhouse or bird feeder, you will be required to saw the wood using two basic cuts—straight and curved. The following paragraphs describe the tools and sawing techniques for making these cuts, as well as methods for making duplicate cuts.

Straight Cuts

The tool of choice for making straight, square, and angled cuts is either a table saw or a radial arm saw. Whichever you choose, make sure it has a high-quality carbide or steel cabinet blade.

The table saw is preferred for making long rips or cutting thin, small pieces. The band saw, if equipped

with a fence and miter gauge, can also be used, although the resulting cut will not be as smooth as a cut made with a circular saw. *A word of warning:* Sawing thin or small pieces can be dangerous with any saw. Fingers get very close to the moving blade. Pieces can jam between the saw and fence and be thrown. Saw from the outside of a larger piece if possible. Get help with cutting if you are not fully familiar with the saw or the proper technique.

If the lumber required is thin (less than ¾ inch), it may be difficult to find at the lumberyard. In that case, resawing will be required; for example, you may have to cut two ¼-inch-thick pieces from one ¾-inch piece. The band saw with a fence and a wide blade is the preferred tool to do this job. A table saw can be used, but the depth of cut is limited (even if you flip the piece over to, in effect, double the depth), and the hazards associated with sawing any thin stock apply. If available, use a planer to obtain the necessary thickness and smooth the surface.

Basic Saw Cuts

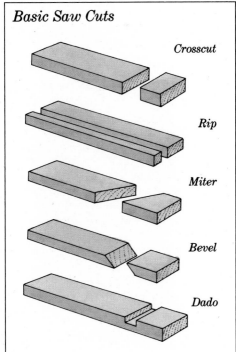

Crosscut

Rip

Miter

Bevel

Dado

If stationary power tools are not available, a handsaw certainly can be used to make many of the required cuts. A jigsaw or saber saw will do the job, but maintaining a straight line is difficult with these tools; you will have to follow up with rasping or sanding. The portable power circular saw can also make many of the cuts.

Curved Cuts

The tool of choice for all outside curved cuts is a stationary power saw, the band saw. Use a narrow blade with fine teeth for the small radius cut. The bench scroll saw is also a good (but slower) choice for both outside and inside cuts.

The hand-held power jigsaw or saber saw is an excellent tool for making curved cuts in stock up to 1½ inches thick. An advantage of this type of saw is the ability to make a plunge cut for saw-blade access for cutting enclosed shapes. If power equipment is not available, the hand-held version of the coping saw works well. Both the coping saw and the scroll saw have removable blades.

Access to an inside cut can be gained by predrilling an access hole, then inserting the saw blade.

Curved Cuts

Jigsaw plunge cut

To make an inside cut without a starter hole, tip the saw forward on the front edge of the shoe so the blade is above the cut line. Start the saw and pivot back and down slowly so the blade cuts into the wood. When the shoe rests firmly on the work, push forward and follow the cut line.

Using an access hole

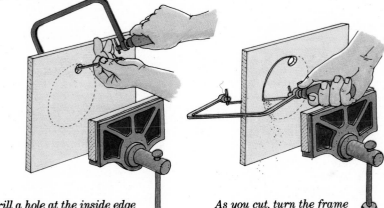

Drill a hole at the inside edge of the cut line. Detach the blade from the saw, pass it through the hole, and reattach it.

As you cut, turn the frame so it is out of the way as you follow the cut line.

The throat depth of the frame of the coping saw, the scroll saw, or the band saw limits the reach to inside cuts. However, this should not be a problem with small projects such as bird feeders or birdhouses.

Duplicate Cuts

A number of the birdhouse and bird feeder designs call for two or more pieces cut to the same pattern. The patterns usually call for curved saw cuts. Frequently, the required pieces can be stacked and gang-cut with a band saw, scroll saw, or jigsaw. The edges can also be gang-sanded. This ensures perfectly matched pieces, and it saves work. The problem is how to hold the pieces firmly while sawing, and then separate them easily with a minimum of damage. There are several ways.

Method 1. Tack the pieces by using fine wire brads. After the pattern is sawed, pull the pieces apart, remove the brads, and fill the holes with wood filler. If possible, position the brad holes in parts of the pieces that will not be visible when the piece is assembled.

Method 2. Use double-stick carpet tape. Most hardware or carpet stores stock it.

Method 3. Use several very small drops of hot-melt glue (from a glue gun). After sawing, the pieces should pry apart easily, with a minimum of damage to the surfaces.

In any case, take care to orient the pieces so that if any damage to the surface occurs from the temporary joining, it will be to the poorer face. As an example, when using ACX (exterior) plywood, match and glue the two C faces together.

Holes

Small holes (½ inch or less) can be easily drilled with an electric hand drill or drill press, using twist drill bits. Brad point bits, if available, are preferred for drilling wood. In any case, use higher speeds when drilling small holes, and, whenever possible, use a backup wood scrap to prevent the drill from tearing the wood when exiting the piece. The projects in this book frequently call for large holes (¾ inch to 3 inches in diameter). These large holes present specific problems and require specific cutting tools. A Forstner bit (also known as a spur bit) or a hole saw work well. An adjustable circle cutter can also do the job. *Caution:* Always secure the circle cutter in a drill press. It is dangerous to use in a hand-held drill. Again, use a backup piece to prevent tearing when the tool emerges.

If a Forstner bit, hole saw, or cutter is not available in the correct diameter, use a jigsaw with a stiff wide blade to make a plunge cut. Then change to a narrow blade to cut the hole. A coping saw or scroll saw are excellent tools for making narrow-radius or delicate inside cuts. When using either tool, begin by drilling an access hole.

Transferring Shapes From Illustrations

You may need to transfer the shapes from the illustrations to your work before sawing them out. Frequently, the outline needs to be enlarged. The time-tested way to do this is to use a grid. Draw the enlarged grid on the work or on a piece of cardboard for a pattern, and transfer the shape, square for square, from the grid on the illustration. The illustrations will tell you what size grid to use.

If the illustration is full size, it can be traced and then transferred to the work using carbon paper or sewing transfer paper. Another method is to photocopy the illustration, cut it out and use it as a pattern. Some photocopy machines will also make enlargements. Because the maximum enlargement is about 150 percent, you may have to make it in two or more steps to reach the desired size.

Kerfing Plywood

Several projects call for bending ¼-inch plywood pieces into curved shapes. To do this, the plywood must be kerfed. Kerfs are a series of closely spaced cross-grained saw cuts that almost—but not completely—cut through the piece.

Use ACX (exterior) plywood for the curved pieces that are to be kerfed. This means that one face has an A-grade veneer and the other a C-grade veneer. The *X* stands for *exterior;* it means the wood can be used outdoors. A-grade is the best veneer. Except for patches (football-shaped inserts), the A face should have no visible defects. Be sure the kerfing is done on the poorer C face.

A table saw or radial arm saw is almost a necessity for kerfing. The table saw is preferred. Use a fairly thick saw blade. The depth of kerf cuts is critical with ½-inch plywood—make them approximately 3/16 inch deep (depending upon the exact thickness of the plywood). If too shallow, the piece won't bend and could break; if too deep, the piece will almost surely break. Saw just deep enough so that the glue line (dark material on the outside top veneer laminate) is showing at the bottom of the kerf. This laminate is thin, a little thicker than 1/16 inch, so be careful. The spacing between the saw cuts should be approximately ½ inch, closer for very sharp bends.

A word of caution if using a table saw: The moving saw blade is hidden when making the cuts, but it is very much there. Be careful with hand position as you push the piece over the saw.

Sanding

Because many of these projects have curved sawn surfaces, coarse (50- to 80-grit) sandpaper or a rasp is needed to remove the saw marks and smooth the curved edges. Before the object is assembled, all surfaces should be lightly sanded with medium (80- to 120-grit) sandpaper to remove the "fuzz," round the edges, and smooth the surfaces. The only objects exempt from the medium-grit sanding are those meant to retain a rough-sawn or barky appearance.

Hand-sanding is laborious at best. If hand-sanding, sanding blocks can make the job easier. There are many types of power sanders available, from inexpensive vibrating-pad sanders to belt and disk sanders. Some are available in stationary and portable versions. Several projects call for the use of a belt sander to put flats on curved arcs. If a belt sander is not available, use a wood rasp.

Mounting Methods

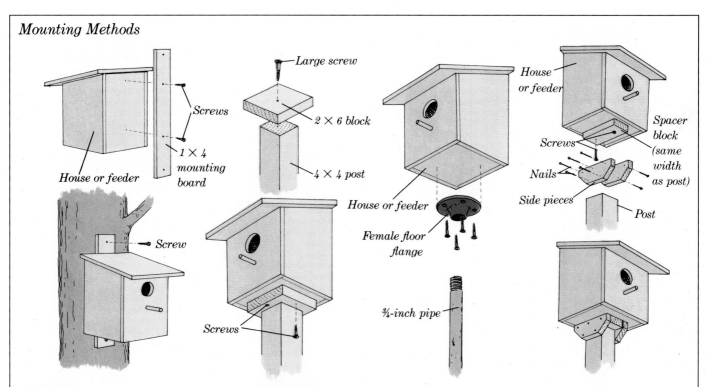

Screws

1 × 4 mounting board

House or feeder

House or feeder

Screw

Large screw

2 × 6 block

4 × 4 post

Screws

House or feeder

Female floor flange

¾-inch pipe

House or feeder

Screws

Nails

Side pieces

Spacer block (same width as post)

Post

Finish

As mentioned previously, the surfaces of cedar and redwood heartwood can be left unfinished; these woods weather nicely. However, any wood will withstand the elements better and look more attractive over time when finished. For cedar or redwood, an exterior oil stain of the kind often used to finish house exteriors or decks is an excellent choice. If the project is made with plywood, exterior paint is the best choice. Using a primer coat helps mask the strong grain. Paint is also the best choice if pine or some other nondurable wood is used.

Whatever finish you choose, apply it to the outside only. Exposure to some finishes and the accompanying fumes can be fatal to birds.

Mounting

All the projects are going to have to be mounted on a tree, building, or post or suspended from an overhang. The best method to mount a birdhouse or feeder against a tree or other object is to use a mounting board, a 1 by 4 or 1 by 6 that is 6 to 8 inches longer than the project. Use screws to fasten the board to the back of the house or feeder, then fasten the board to the mounting surface by using screws or nails.

If post-mounted, a mounting block or blocks are needed. The simplest is a piece of 1 by 6 or 2 by 6 that is nailed or lagged (that is, attached by a large screw) onto the end of the post. Then, screwing from the bottom of the block up through your project, attach the house or feeder to the block. A better post mount is made of several side pieces of wood and a spacer block. After attaching the spacer to the bottom of the house or feeder, use screws or nails to fasten the side pieces to the sides of the post.

Another way of post mounting uses steel pipe. The best pipe for this purpose is ½- or ¾-inch pipe that is threaded on one end. Be sure the pipe is galvanized to prevent rusting. Screw a female floor flange to the end of the pipe. Then drive the other end into the ground, being careful not to damage the flange. Remove the flange and use four 1-inch plated screws to attach it to the bottom of the house or feeder. Screw the flange back on to the end of the post, and the mounting is complete.

If the feeder or birdhouse is to be mounted on a wood post set in the ground, the wood must be pressure-treated to protect it from rot. Pressure-treated 4 by 4s are readily available and are an excellent choice.

Some feeders can be hung from a branch or overhang. Place one or more screw eyes in the top of the feeder; use a configuration that allows the feeder to hang level. Suspend the feeder by attaching synthetic line or galvanized wire.

MATERIALS

Only wood should be used to build birdhouses. Plastic or metal most probably will not be used by nesting birds. These materials provide a potential for heat build-up that could damage eggs and kill newly hatched chicks. Bird feeders should also be constructed of wood because (even if painted) the wood at a feeding platform provides birds with a better surface to grip while feeding.

The following section describes the kinds of wood and other materials needed to build your projects.

Woods

Many of the common framing or construction woods—such as Douglas fir, southern yellow pine, and hemlock—are coarse, grainy, and split easily. Unless treated, they are not durable. For birdhouses and bird feeders, you need an even-textured, split-resistant, weather-resistant wood that is easy to cut, shape, and work.

Because all these projects are for outside use, the woods of choice are western red cedar or redwood. These woods provide weather resistance, are easy to work, and can be found in larger widths that are relatively free of knots and other defects. Both accept a finish; if left unfinished, they weather attractively.

Select redwood or cedar that has a preponderance of heartwood (darker wood). The soft pines—including white pine, Ponderosa (western yellow) pine, and sugar pine—are also acceptable choices. Spruce and the wood of true firs are acceptable if the wood is of high quality. Soft pine, spruce, and fir do not have the outdoor durability of cedar or redwood, however. They must be well finished with an exterior paint or oil stain.

Whatever wood you choose, be careful that it is reasonably dry. Otherwise, you may have glue failure, the wood may shrink and warp, and the finish may end up with blemishes.

If you use plywood, the best choice is marine-grade plywood. Unfortunately, this type is frequently unavailable and usually expensive. The next best choice is ACX (exterior) plywood. The more common exterior construction grade, CDX, is made of Douglas fir or southern yellow pine. These woods are coarse, split easily, vary in thickness, and frequently have internal voids. Strand board or waferboard would work but are not preferred choices; particleboard and hardboard would produce satisfactory results. In any case make sure you use dry exterior-grade wood.

Barky Wood

The Bluebird Tree House and the Screech-Owl Box lend themselves to a rustic exterior using barky wood.

There are two sources for the bark: You can use slabwood, the first slice of lumber that comes directly from the barky outside of the log, or fasten bark from another source to the already constructed house.

The best choice is slabwood. The best place to get slabwood is at a small local sawmill. To find one, look in the yellow pages under *custom sawing.* Don't go to a larger sawmill—they debark their logs before sawing, and the bark is shredded in the process. If the slabs come from logs cut in the spring, when the sap is running, the bark will slip and come off easily. However, it can be tacked on to prevent this.

Slabwood will undoubtedly be green, and it will shrink in use. Shrinkage might loosen the bark, so tack it on. Glue will not bond well, so use extra nails in assembly. Slabwood thickness varies considerably. However, with a little searching, some usable pieces should be found.

If no slabwood is available, strip bark off a piece of firewood or some other available source, then attach the bark to the assembled birdhouse. Firewood freshly cut in the spring is the best source if you are peeling bark. The bark should slip off easily. If it holds tightly, the bark usually breaks when an attempt is made to remove it. If stuck, prolonged soaking may help. Try warm water. Bark tightness varies tremendously with species as well as with the season in which the tree is cut.

As soon as the bark is removed and starts to dry, it will start to curl. Press it flat, put a heavy object on it, and let it dry until you are ready to attach it to the birdhouse. If already curled, try soaking the bark pieces. This will soften them and reduce the chance of splitting or breaking when fastened to the house.

Lumber sizes. Surfaced or planed boards sold as 1 by 4s, 2 by 4s, 2 by 6s, and so forth are not really the advertised size. All are anywhere from ¼ to ⅝ inch undersize. For instance, when dry, a 1 by 4 is ¾ inch by 3½ inches; a 1 by 12 is ¾ inch by 11¼ inches; and so on. If the wood is green, the actual size may be slightly thicker and wider than if the lumber were dry. Actual plywood thicknesses are the same as the advertised size—that is, ¼-inch plywood is exactly ¼ inch thick.

Several projects call for very thin or narrow pieces for edging, rails, trim, and the like. These can be sawn from larger pieces but—again—if you use a power saw, do it with care. Fingers get very close to moving blades. As an alternative to cutting,

Lumber Sizes

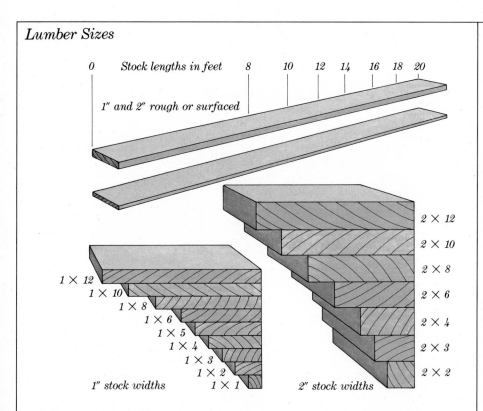

look through the molding bins at your lumber or building-supply store. You may find ready-made molding that you can use. Hobby shops are also good sources for obtaining thin and narrow stock.

If larger pieces of thin (less than ¾ inch) solid wood stock are called for in a project, it may be difficult to find on the shelf at the lumberyard. You may have to reduce 1-inch lumber (¾ inch thick) to the needed thickness. There are several ways to do this.

• See if your lumberyard has a planer or resaw. For a fee the lumberyard might machine the stock to the required thickness.

• Take purchased ¾-inch material to a cabinet shop. Most have planers and resawing equipment and are willing to do custom work.

• Do the job yourself, using your own or a friend's woodworking equipment. The needed thickness can be obtained either by planing a thicker piece down to the required thickness or by resawing. If you use a planer on stock greater than ⅜ inch thick, make several passes, surfacing the lumber

down to the final thickness. If material less than ⅜ inch is required, it is most economical to first resaw the ¾-inch stock, ripping it on edge in half, and then planing to the final thickness.

If a planer is not available, you can obtain the required thickness simply by sawing. The band saw with a fence and wide blade is the preferred (and safest) tool to do this job. It will leave a rough face that will have to be smoothed by sanding.

A table saw can be used, but the depth of the cut is limited (although you can flip the piece over to, in effect, double the depth of the cut). Use the smoothest-cut rip or combination blade you have. Of course, with either band or table saw, first rip the piece(s) to the minimum width needed to keep the depth of the cut to a minimum.

If you do this on either power saw, take special caution—there will be a lot of blade exposed. The use of a push stick is mandatory. With the

table saw, hold-downs should also be used. Beware of the thin piece getting caught between the saw and fence and being thrown. A radial arm saw should not be used for any ripping operations involving thin or narrow stock.

Glue

Nailing is adequate; nailing and gluing are better. Because all the projects presented in this book are for outdoor use, you need waterproof glue. The common white and yellow wood glues (polyvinyl and aliphatic resin products) are not weatherproof; given time, they will fail when wet. Urea formaldehyde resin glue, which you buy in a powder and mix with water, is better than a common glue. Still, it is not completely waterproof. The best waterproof glue is the kind you mix yourself by combining a liquid resin and a catalyst powder. This type of glue is called a resorcinol resin glue. The glue is strong and waterproof, but it has disadvantages. It is unhandy to use, has a short pot life, and leaves a dark purple stain wherever applied. As an alternative, epoxy glue is fine for small pieces. Silicone sealer can serve as a waterproof glue, but it is not very strong. It might work well enough when used in conjunction with nails. Check at your favorite hardware store. New glues are coming on the market all the time, and you might find the very product you need.

Hardware

Projects for the outdoors call for exterior hardware. Nails and brads should be galvanized or otherwise plated or coated to prevent rusting. Aluminum or brass nails are an appropriate choice. Nails for plasterboard are for interior use and usually have no protective coating. When it comes to screws, use brass screws as much as possible. Hooks, eyes, and other hardware should also be brass, or at the least, brass-plated.

CONSTRUCTING BIRDHOUSES

This chapter presents 12 birdhouse-building projects. Each project is named after a common backyard species. With luck, your new birdhouse will attract that species. However, different species of birds may find the birdhouse to their liking, especially if it meets their requirements for size, shelter, and proximity to a desirable and safe habitat. This is no cause for alarm or discouragement. Such an event should be looked upon as fortuitous, for all feathered visitors to the backyard should be welcomed and enjoyed. If the birdhouse name does not match the birdhouse residents, the simple solution is to rename the birdhouse after the resident species. The birds won't mind a bit.

A birdhouse should take advantage of the surrounding habitat as much as possible. This nesting box, designed to attract Wood Ducks, is properly placed near a pond bordered by trees.

HOUSE FINCH COUNTRY HOME

T he warbling songs of the House Finch are a welcome sound in any backyard. In the West it isn't uncommon to find the nest of this bird in a cactus. They are equally at home in the country or in town and readily adapt to their environment. This country home birdhouse will be well used—this species normally produces two broods per year.

Description and Tool Requirements

This project is relatively straightforward and simple. You can construct it by using hand tools alone, but a radial arm or table saw would greatly facilitate sawing—especially when it comes to the angled roof cuts. To build this birdhouse, you need a drill with ⅛-, ¼-, and ½-inch drill bits, as well as a 2-inch Forstner bit, hole saw, or circle cutter. If these cutters are not available, the entrance hole can be sawn out with a coping saw or scroll saw.

Two or more bar clamps or pipe clamps will be needed when you glue the roof base. A belt sander would be useful for giving the final shape to and smoothing the laminated roof.

Building Steps

1. Begin by sawing the sides. Cut two 6- by 6¾-inch pieces from the 1 by 8 board. Then cut one 6¾- by 7½-inch piece to serve as the back.

2. Measure and cut the bottom first, which should be 6 by 9½ inches, and then the front, which should be 6 by 11½ inches.

3. As a break from sawing, bore or cut the holes. Drill four ½-inch holes in the back to serve as air vents. Drill five ½-inch drainage holes in the bottom. The 2-inch entrance hole is either bored or sawn from the front piece. Use the illustrations to carefully place these holes (see "Building

Basics," page 22, for discussion of how to make holes).

4. Now, back to the saw. The roof is composed of 5 separate pieces of lumber cut to form a pyramid. The largest piece, the bottom of the pyramid, must be edge-glued from 2 pieces of the 1 by 8. Saw 2 pieces approximately 10 inches long. Rip a 2-inch strip from one piece. Using the bar clamps, edge-glue these pieces to double the width. Waterproof glue should be used, (see "Building Basics," page 25, for discussion of gluing).

5. While the glue is drying, you will cut the other roof pieces. This job is best done with a radial arm or table

The adaptable House Finch should find this a comfortable nesting place to produce its two annual broods of chicks.

House Finch Country Home

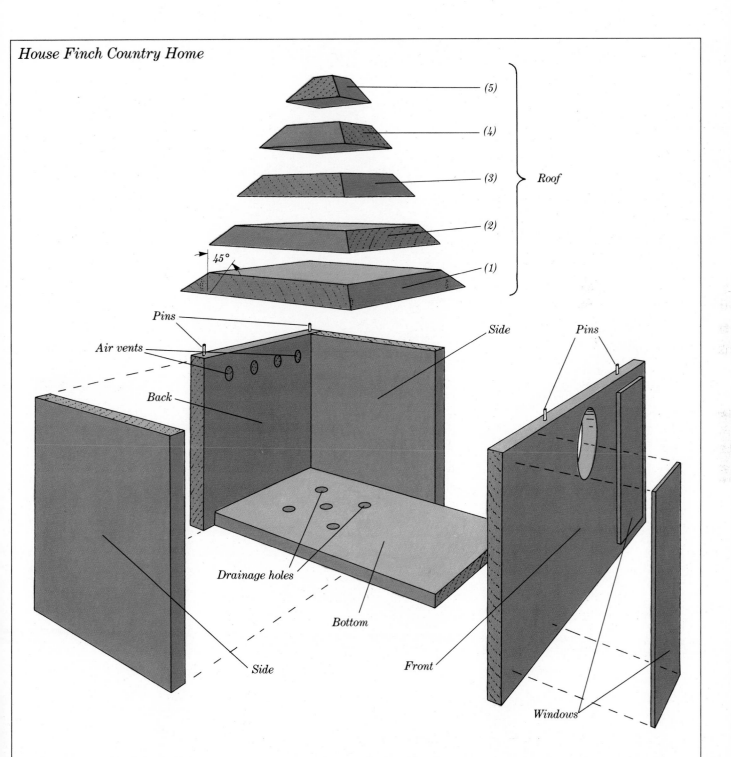

(5)

(4)

(3) — *Roof*

(2)

45° — *(1)*

Pins

Air vents

Back

Side

Pins

Side

Drainage holes

Bottom

Front

Windows

saw set to cut a 45-degree angle. (With a table saw, make these cuts with the fence to the left of the saw blade.) Cut one 7-inch square, one 5½-inch square, one 4-inch square, and one 2½-inch square. Take care in sawing the 45-degree bias cut,

whether using the radial arm or the table saw. Especially with the smaller pieces, watch your fingers and be alert to the possibility of the saw throwing the pieces. As soon as the largest roof section is dry, cut it to form an 8½-inch square.

6. Now you will cut the decorative "windows." Make these from ¼-inch plywood scrap or from thin exterior hardboard.

7. Now preassemble everything to make sure of the fit. When everything does fit, assemble the main body of

the birdhouse by using the waterproof glue and the 1½-inch finishing nails. Countersink the nails and, if desired, use wood filler to fill the part of the hole that remains visible. When the filler dries, sand it flush with the surface.

8. In this step you will use the waterproof glue and the 1½-inch finishing nails to assemble the roof pieces, which will take the shape of a pyramid. To prevent the small pieces from splitting when nailed, predrill the nail holes by using a drill bit slightly smaller than the shafts of the nails. Apply the glue to the 8½-inch roof piece. Place the 7-inch roof piece on top of it, and fasten the pieces with the 1½-inch nails. Continue gluing and nailing the roof pieces until the pyramid is completed. Use clamps, if necessary, to hold the pieces tightly.

9. After the glue has fully dried, sand the body and roof, removing "fuzz," rounding the edges, and smoothing the surfaces. A belt sander would be useful in providing a final smooth shape to the roof. If a belt sander is not available, use a wood rasp or sanding block.

10. In this step you will attach the decorative windows in the positions shown in the photograph (page 29). Apply the waterproof glue, position each window, and use brads to attach them to the front.

11. Now you will place the roof on the house. It will be removable for cleaning. Start by driving the 2-inch finishing nails about ¾ inch into each of the 4 corners. Clip off the heads at a bias to leave a sharp end. Now, carefully position the roof above the

Materials List

All the solid wood pieces can be cut from a piece of surfaced 1 by 8 approximately 8 feet long. Choose any soft-textured pine, cedar, or redwood. Select a piece with few knots or with clear space between the defects. (See "Building Basics," page 24, for discussion of materials.)

Lumber

Piece	No. of Pieces	Thickness	Width	Length
Sides	2	¾"	6"	6¾"
Back	1	¾"	6¾"	7½"
Bottom	1	¾"	6"	9½"
Front	1	¾"	6"	11½"
Roof (1) (edge-glued)	1	¾"	8½"	8½"
Roof (2)	1	¾"	7"	7"
Roof (3)	1	¾"	5½"	5½"
Roof (4)	1	¾"	4"	4"
Roof (5)	1	¾"	2½"	2½"
Windows*	2	⅛"–¼"	2¼"	4½"

Mounting block(s) or board (see discussion of mounting, page 23).
*Any small thin pieces, such as ¼" plywood or ⅛" hardboard, will suffice for the windows.

Hardware and Miscellaneous

Item	Quantity	Size	Description
Finishing nails	20	1½"	Galvanized or aluminum
Finishing nails	4	2"	Galvanized or aluminum
Brads	10	½"–1"	Brass, if available
Glue	1 small can		Waterproof
Sandpaper		80–120 grit	Medium
Primer	1 pint		Exterior
Finish	1 pint		Exterior oil stain or paint
Mounting screws	4	2" × #8	Brass, round head
Wood filler	¼ pint		

house, resting the roof on the nails. Gently tap on the roof just hard enough so the nail ends leave marks in the bottom of the roof. At each nail mark drill into the roof with a drill bit slightly larger than the nails. Use a stop so the drill does not penetrate through to the top surface. Now place the roof on top of the birdhouse. If needed, bend any nail slightly to make the roof fit. Clip the top off any nail that is too long, and file the sharp ends. The roof should be easy to remove, but tight enough so it will not blow off.

12. Basic assembly is now finished. If you wish, add more decorative touches such as a chimney or planter boxes under the windows. Now add a finish to the exterior of the house. If you decide to use stain, choose an

exterior oil stain. If you choose to paint, apply a primer coat to fill in the end grain of the roof. Then apply a high-quality enamel paint. Choose a natural or soft color; generally, birds are not attracted to bright colors.

13. The last step is mounting. Because of the roof overhang, the House Finch Country Home is best mounted from the base. Following the instructions in "Building Basics" (page 23), fashion a mounting block or a combination of spacer block and mounting boards; the mounting surface will determine the mounting device to use.

FLYCATCHER CHALET

This chalet will welcome woodpeckers, Tree Swallows, or bluebirds as well as flycatchers.

T he Great Crested Flycatcher is a fierce and aggressive protector of its territory. This bird can startle even a human intruder with its shrill cry. Although this chalet birdhouse was designed especially to attract this bird and its mate, other birds that may nest in it include Downy Woodpeckers, Tree Swallows, or bluebirds.

Description and Tool Requirements

This is a straightforward and simple-to-build birdhouse with some curves and trim to give it charm. A table or radial arm saw would make cutting the angles easy. A jigsaw or band saw is needed for the curved cuts, and a drill with $5/32$- and $1/2$-inch bits is needed. The 2-inch entrance hole can be made with a circle cutter or hole saw; or, saw it with a jigsaw (see "Building Basics," pages 18–22, for discussion of tools and techniques for cutting).

This birdhouse can be mounted either on a post- or back-mounted against a tree (see "Building Basics," page 23, for mounting techniques). The bottom is removable for cleaning. The materials list does not include wood for mounting, because mounting pieces easily can be made from scraps.

Materials List

Soft wood—such as Ponderosa pine, white pine, or sugar pine—will work fine for this project. If a natural finish is desired, use western red cedar. Whatever the wood, a piece of surfaced 1 by 8, 6 to 8 feet long, should be sufficient. Get a reasonably defect-free wood. When sawing, cut the chalet pieces from between any knots. Some scraps of thin plywood or hardboard are used for the "windows." (See "Building Basics," page 24, for discussion of materials.)

Lumber

Piece	No. of Pieces	Thickness	Width	Length
Sides	2	¾″	6″	9″
Roof	2	¾″	6½″	10″
Front and back ends	2	¾″	7½″	10″
Base	1	¾″	7½″	9″
Porch	2	¾″	1½″	2″
Railings	2	⅛″	⅜″	7½″

Hardware and Miscellaneous

Item	Quantity	Size	Description
Finishing nails	12	⅝″	Galvanized or aluminum
Finishing nails	20	1½″	Galvanized or aluminum
Glue	1 small can		Waterproof
Sandpaper		80–120 grit	Medium
Finish	1 pint		Exterior oil stain or paint
Mounting screws	4	1½″ × #8	Brass, round head
Wood filler	½ pint		

Building Steps

1. Using a radial arm or table saw, square cut the 2 sides, roof pieces, and front and back ends. Saw the base piece and the 2 porch sides to dimension. From scraps of plywood or hardboard, saw the railings. Be careful with these small pieces; fingers get very close to the moving saw. (Read about sawing thin stock in "Building Basics," page 20.)

2. Now set the saw angle to 28 degrees and cut a bevel on one edge of each roof piece and each side. (Instead of a saw, a jointer can be used for this operation.)

3. Draw the gable roof lines on the front and back pieces. If using a table saw, set the miter gauge at 62 degrees (90 degrees minus 28 degrees). Set a radial arm saw to 28 degrees. Make the 2 sloping roof cuts on both ends.

Flycatcher Chalet

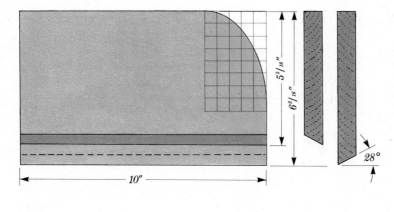

Roof pieces (make 2 different widths)

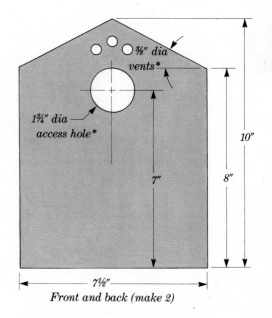

Front and back (make 2)

*Vents in back only; access hole in front only

4. The last sawing operation consists of cutting the curved fronts of the roof. Trace the pattern from the drawing onto one of the pieces, using a grid if necessary. Temporarily join the two roof pieces together for gang-sawing (see "Building Basics," page 21, for duplicate cutting techniques). Saw the curves with a jigsaw or band saw. Sand the edges smooth, then separate the pieces.

5. Lay out the entrance hole in the front piece, using the dimensions shown on the illustrations (page 32). The entrance hole should be centered and 7 inches from the bottom. Use a 1¾-inch bit or hole saw, if available. Otherwise, saw the hole by using a coping saw, scroll saw, or jigsaw. As shown in the illustration, drill three ⅜-inch vent holes in the upper part of the back piece. (Refer to the discussion of holes in "Building Basics," page 22.)

6. Now is a good time to get most of the sanding done. Using wood filler, fill any external defects. After the filler is dry, sand smooth the surfaces of all the pieces, and round the edges and corners.

7. Assemble the pieces and check for proper fit. When the fit is correct, glue and nail the front, back, sides, and roof pieces. For fasteners, use 1½-inch finishing nails. Do not attach the base at this time.

8. The base will be fastened to the bottom of the house with screws, so the base can be removed for cleaning. Because of this the base and porch parts are assembled separately. Attach the 2 porch sides to the front of the base, gluing and nailing up from the bottom. Check the illustration (page 33) for the correct position. You may want to use smaller brads for this to prevent the nails from splitting the porch side blocks. Use clamps while the glue is drying.

9. After the glue has set, remove the clamps and move the base to the edge of your workbench. Using the ⅝-inch finishing nails, attach the

Flycatcher Chalet

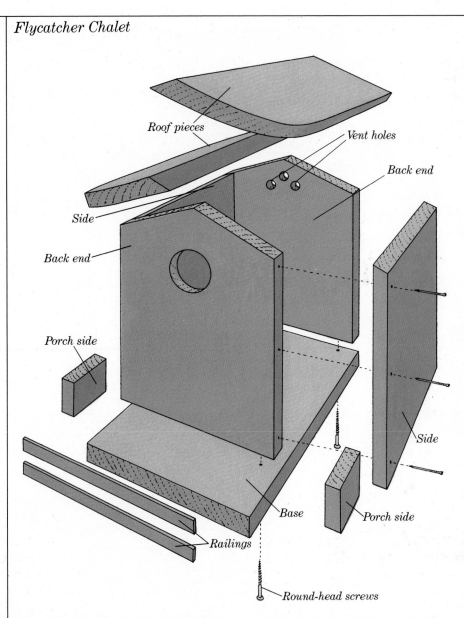

Roof pieces
Vent holes
Back end
Side
Back end
Porch side
Side
Base
Porch side
Railings
Round-head screws

railings to the porch sides. See the illustration for details.

10. Predrill ⁵/₃₂-inch screw pilot holes in the base (check the illustrations for exact placement). Using mounting screws, fasten the base assembly onto the bottom of the house.

11. You may want to countersink and fill all the nail holes with wood filler. When the filler has dried, sand the filler flush with the wood surface. Give the entire house a final once-over with sandpaper.

12. If cedar was used, an oil stain on the outside will be attractive and provide the necessary weather protection. If you paint the outside of the chalet with exterior paint, the color should be dull. Avoid very bright colors; they repel some birds.

13. The Flycatcher Chalet should be mounted from the back, using a mounting board to permit access for cleaning (see "Building Basics," page 23, for mounting techniques).

TREE SWALLOW HOUSE

U nlike other swallows, the Tree Swallow has readily adapted to birdhouses, especially ones near large or small bodies of water, marshes, or wet meadows. Tree Swallows are quite tolerant of close neighbors of their own species. You may try mounting two boxes near each other or even in the same tree. The Tree Swallow birdhouse is the ideal size for this popular bird.

Description and Tool Requirements

The bent plywood sides and roof and the curved trim make this birdhouse interesting to build. Hand tools, including a saber saw or jigsaw, can do most of the job, but a band saw would make cutting the curves somewhat easier. A radial arm or table saw is necessary to kerf the bent side and roof piece (see ''Building Basics,'' page 22, for discussions of tools and kerfing).

Tree Swallows adapt readily to birdhouses, especially if they are located near water.

A drill with ⅛-, ¼-, and ⅜-inch drill bits is needed. Drilling the entrance hole requires a 1½-inch spade or Forstner bit. If a 1½-inch bit is unavailable, a hole saw or circle cutter can do the job. Another alternative is to saw the hole by using a coping or scroll saw. The project also requires some medium-size clamps.

The Tree Swallow House should be mounted from the back, using a mounting board (see "Building Basics," page 23, for discussion of mounting techniques).

Building Steps

1. You will begin by cutting the two 10-inch pieces from the 1 by 8 pine. These pieces will be the front and back of the house. If you have a band saw or a large jigsaw with narrow blades, duplicate cutting will save you time. Using a grid, transfer the pattern from the illustration (page 35) onto one of the blanks. Temporarily join the blanks for duplicate cutting, and gang-saw the pieces (see "Building Basics," page 21, for discussion of duplicate cutting). If you don't have the tools for duplicate cutting, trace the pattern twice and cut the pieces separately.

After the pieces have been sawn to shape, sand the curved edges. A belt or drum sander would be useful for this. If the pieces were joined for duplicate cutting, separate the pieces after sanding.

2. Now prepare to cut two 2- by 7-inch pieces from the ¾-inch pine to form the overhang. As before, trace the pattern from the illustration onto one or both pieces. If possible, temporarily join the pieces and gang-saw them; or, cut each piece separately. Sand the edges and, if necessary, separate the pieces.

Tree Swallow House

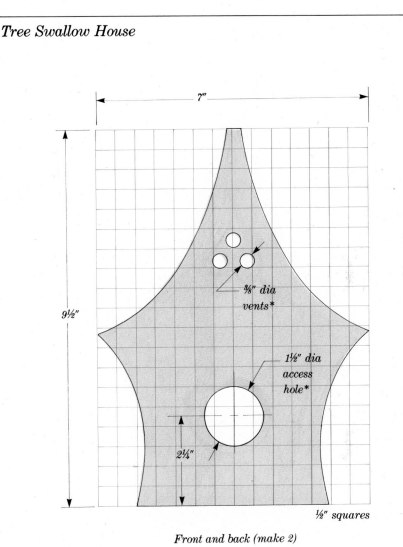

7″

9½″

⅜″ dia vents*

1½″ dia access hole*

2¼″

½″ squares

Front and back (make 2)

Access hole in front only; vent holes in back only

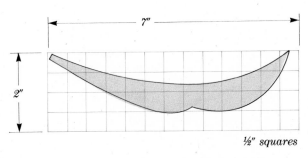

7″

2″

½″ squares

Overhang trim (make 2)

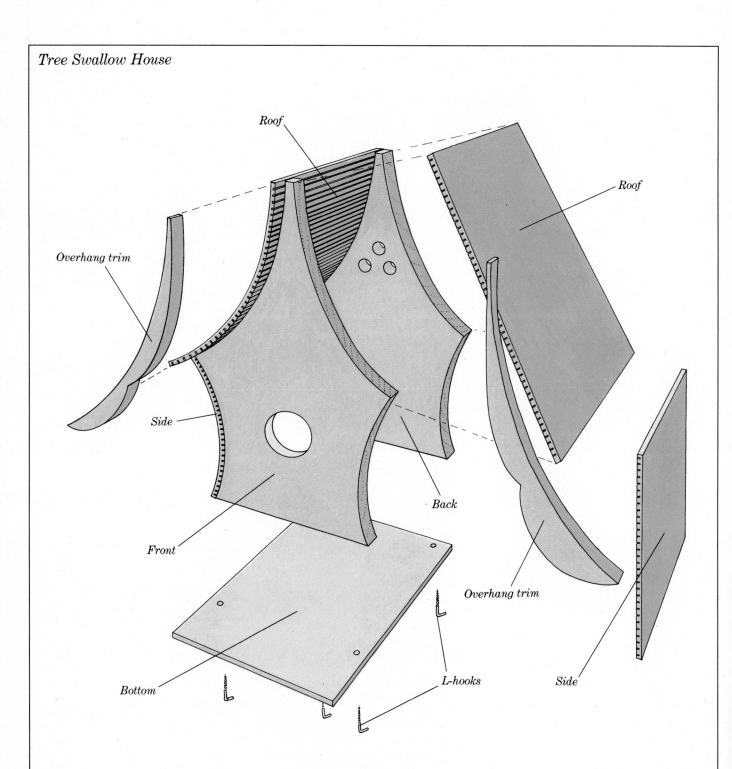

Roof

Roof

Overhang trim

Side

Back

Front

Overhang trim

Bottom

L-hooks

Side

3. Bring your piece of ¼-inch plywood to the saw. Be sure the outside grain is running lengthwise. Saw from a portion of the plywood that has a clear, straight-grained face with no patches or defects. Cut out the 2 roof pieces and the 2 side pieces. then cut the piece that will serve as the floor of the birdhouse.

4. While you are still at the saw, kerf the roof and side pieces so they can be bent to the desired shape (see "Building Basics," page 22, for a discussion of kerfing). Note: Practice

Materials List

ACX (exterior) ¼-inch sanded plywood is the principal construction material. A piece of plywood approximately 1 foot by 3 feet should be more than ample for all the required pieces. A 2-foot piece of 1 by 8 surfaced soft pine should provide all the other pieces required. (See "Building Basics," page 24, for discussion of materials.)

Lumber

Piece	No. of Pieces	Thickness	Width	Length
Front and back	2	¾"	7½"	10"
Overhang trim	2	¾"	2"	7"
Roof pieces	2	¼"	7⅜"	7⅜"
Sides	2	¼"	4⅛"	7⅜"
Floor	1	¼"	5⅜"	8¼"
Mounting board	1	¾"	3½"	12"

Hardware and Miscellaneous

Item	Quantity	Size	Description
Finishing nails	30 (approx.)	¾"	Galvanized or aluminum
Glue	¼ cup		Waterproof
Sandpaper		80–120 grit	Medium
Finish	1 pint		Exterior primer and paint
Wood filler	¼ pint		
Screw L-hooks	4	⅛" × 1"	Brass or plated
Mounting screws	4	1¼" × #8	Brass, flat head

kerfing a piece of scrap before you try kerfing the plywood pieces. Check the depth of cut, spacing, ease of bending, and so on.

5. Now, before you start the assembly, you will need to bore or saw all the holes. Place the entrance hole and the vent holes in the locations shown in the illustration (page 35). First drill three ⅜-inch ventilation holes in the top of the back piece. Be sure to use a piece of scrap wood for backup to prevent the drill from splitting the wood when it emerges.

Swallows need a 1½-inch entrance hole. Position the entrance hole according to the illustration (page 35). If available, use a Forstner bit or 1½-inch spade bit to bore the entrance. A circle cutter or hole saw will also do the job. (Be sure to use the circle cutter in a drill press. It is dangerous to use with a hand drill.) Again, use a backup to prevent splitting.

An alternative to boring the entrance hole is to saw it. After drawing the circle with a drawing compass, predrill a ¼-inch saw-access hole. Then carefully saw the entrance circles with a coping saw or scroll saw. If needed, the round side of a wood rasp can be used for shaping and smoothing the hole.

Finally, drill ⅛-inch holes in the 4 corners of the floor, as shown in the illustrations (page 36).

6. Preassemble the pieces to check the fit. Glue and nail the overhang trim pieces to the front. Let the glue dry thoroughly.

7. Test the side pieces to see if they bend easily to the shape of the ends. If they resist, don't force; try soaking the pieces in cold water to make them pliable. Don't use hot water or prolong the soaking—the plywood could delaminate. (If you think even cold water could harm the wood, try soaking a piece of scrap.) To ensure a strong bond, let the pieces partially dry before gluing.

Apply glue. Then start bending the side pieces, one at a time, into the curved front and back pieces, nailing them in place as you go. Use clamps if necessary. The sides should be flush with the edges of the sanded front piece and the back piece; see the illustration (page 36).

8. After the glued sides are dry, glue and nail the roof pieces in the same manner as the sides. Again, use clamps if necessary, and keep checking the illustration for position. Allow the glue to dry thoroughly.

9. With wood filler and a putty knife, fill in the exposed kerf slots and any other open spaces and cracks. Take care not to overdo the filling; excess filler will just have to be sanded off.

10. When the filler is completely dry, give everything a good sanding, removing "fuzz," rounding edges and corners, and smoothing the various surfaces.

11. Give the outside of the house a coating of exterior primer paint. When the primer is dry, paint it with a dull enamel. Choose green, brown, or some other dull color; avoid using bright colors, some birds don't like them.

12. Attach the bottom by using 4 screw L-hooks. These fasteners will enable you to remove the bottom for cleaning; you won't even need a screwdriver to open the house.

13. Attach a mounting board to the back of the Tree Swallow House (see "Building Basics," page 23, for mounting techniques).

ROBIN'S ROOST

This rustic structure may not look like a birdhouse, but robins like nesting in the open, in the crotch of a tree, or the fork of a branch. They will not nest in a conventional enclosed birdhouse. The Robin's Roost is just the sort of nest site they like. With some modification the same design can be used as a bird feeder.

Description and Tool Requirements

This is a fairly easy project and can be built with basic hand tools. If available, a radial arm or table saw would make cutting easier (see "Building Basics," pages 18–22, for discussion about tools and techniques).

Building Steps

1. First verify that the width of the 1 by 12 is 11¼ inches. If needed, rip the piece to the required width (see "Building Basics," page 24, for discussion of lumber sizes). If the piece happens to be green, then the width may be slightly greater. Saw the back piece from the 1 by 12; the back should be 12 inches long. If a table or radial arm saw is used, saw one cut with a bevel of 30 degrees.

2. Now you will cut the 2 roof pieces from the 1 by 12 cut to 11¼ inches. Rip one piece 5 inches wide and the other 6⅛ inches wide.

3. From a knot-free section of the stock saw the 6- by 8-inch bottom.

4. Cut the 2 roof supports at the angles shown in the illustration (page

39). If using a table saw, set the angles on the miter gauge. On the radial arm saw, the angle is set on the arm. If hand-sawing, trace a pattern onto the wood or use a protractor to mark off the angles.

5. Saw the 2 triangular back braces. Use the same sawing techniques discussed in step 4.

6. Piece together the entire project to check dimensions and fit. If correct, then apply glue and nail the roof pieces together, using at least 5 nails. Clean off any excess glue to prevent it from staining the wood.

7. In this step you will finish the roof assembly by attaching the roof supports. Apply glue, then position them 1 inch from the outside edge of the roof; nail the sides into place. Use at least 4 nails on each side.

8. Next, apply glue where the bottom should meet the back. Align the bottom and the back, then nail the pieces, using at least 5 nails.

9. The next step will be to attach the back braces. To prevent the triangular pieces from splitting, predrill the nail holes with a bit slightly smaller than the shank of the nails. Apply glue where the braces will meet the house, then nail the pieces into place.

10. You will complete the roost by attaching the roof assembly to the back. Apply glue where the 2 pieces should meet. Carefully align the roof and back. First nail from the roof into the back, then nail the back to the roof supports. Use 4 nails for the roof-back connection, and hammer in several more nails into each roof support.

Robins will not use a birdhouse, preferring a ledge or roost on which to build their deep-cup nests.

Robin's Roost

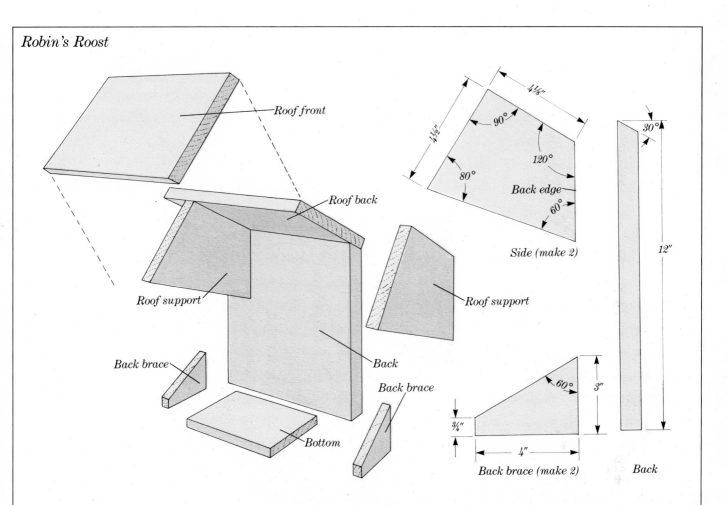

Roof front

Roof back

Roof support

Roof support

Back brace

Back

Back brace

Bottom

Side (make 2)

4⅛″

4½″

90°

80°

120°

Back edge

60°

30°

12″

60°

3″

¾″

4″

Back brace (make 2)

Back

11. Lightly sand the complete assembly to remove "fuzz" and slightly round all edges and corners.

12. If redwood or cedar is used, the project can be left unfinished to weather naturally. An oil stain on the outside of the house would contribute to its longevity and enhance long-term appearance. If pine or other nondurable wood is used, an exterior oil finish or paint is mandatory.

13. To mount the project, drive screws through the back or through the base; the site you choose for the roost determines screw placement (see "Building Basics," page 23, for mounting techniques). Predrill the screw holes to avoid splitting.

Materials List

The Robin's Roost is cut from a 1 by 12, rough sawn or surfaced. Choose western red cedar, redwood, pine, or a similar softwood. You need approximately 3 feet of knot-free material.

Lumber

Piece	No. of Pieces	Thickness	Width	Length
Back	1	¾″	11¼″	12″
Roof back	1	¾″	5″	11¼″
Roof front	1	¾″	6⅛″	11¼″
Bottom	1	¾″	6″	8″
Roof supports	2	¾″	6″	6″
Back braces	2	¾″	3⅝″	4″

Hardware and Miscellaneous

Item	Quantity	Size	Description
Finishing nails	40 (approx.)	2″	Galvanized or aluminum
Glue	1 small can		Waterproof
Sandpaper		80–120 grit	Medium
Finish	1 pint		Exterior oil stain or paint
Mounting screws	2	2″ × #8	Brass, round head

WREN APARTMENT HOUSE

N o other wild bird has taken so completely to birdhouses as the little House Wren. This birdhouse has two "apartments." The chimney hides the ventilation holes. The curvature of the roof tends to discourage would-be predators.

Description and Tool Requirements

The bent plywood roof makes this birdhouse interesting to build. Hand tools, including a jigsaw or saber saw, can do most of the job; but a radial arm or table saw are necessary to kerf the roof piece. A drill with ¼-, ¾-, and 1-inch drill bits is also needed. If a 1-inch bit is not available, the entrance hole can be sawn with a coping or scroll saw (see "Building Basics," page 18, for discussion of tool requirements).

Building Steps

1. From the plywood cut two 7- by 14-inch blanks. From these blanks you will cut the front and back ends. Temporarily join the blanks for gang-sawing (see "Building Basics," page 21, for techniques). If you join the blanks by using a few drops of hot-melt glue, be sure the poorer sides are face to face. Using a compass (or a pencil tied to a string anchored by a tack) draw the 13¾-inch-diameter half-circle on the top blank. (The radius of the circle should be 6⅞ inches.)

The male House Wren often attracts two mates. This apartment house provides shelter for two nesting females and their broods.

2. Saw the arcs, using a jigsaw, saber saw, or—if available—a band saw. Use a fine-cut blade. A coping saw can be used if power saws are not available. While the pieces are still together, sand the sawn edges smooth. Then separate the two pieces. If the glue tears a little grain, that face can go inside when it is ready to be assembled.

3. Now cut the 6⅜- by 13¾-inch bottom piece from the ¼-inch plywood. Refer to the illustration (page 42) to learn the position and size of the two cutouts in the bottom piece. (The cutouts will accommodate the cleanout inserts.) Draw the cutouts on the piece, drill a hole inside each cutout, then cut the openings with a jigsaw. If a jigsaw is not available, use a coping saw or scroll saw.

4. The roof comes next. Select a piece that has a clear, straight-grained face with no patches or defects. Be sure the grain runs lengthwise. Cut the 7- by 23-inch roof piece. Then, using a radial arm or table saw, make multiple parallel saw cuts (kerfs) across the poorer face of the plywood. This side should be up on a radial arm saw, down on a table saw. (See "Building Basics," page 22, for details about kerfing.)

5. The cleanout floor inserts are two pairs of different sized rectangles. The size of the rectangles in the first pair should be 3½ by 4¾ inches; cut the two rectangles. The rectangles in the second pair should be 4½ by 6 inches; cut these two rectangles.

6. While at the saw, you will finish cutting the pieces. Cut the chimney from a piece of 2 by 4 lumber; the chimney should be 2½ inches long. Cut the chimney cover, or cap, from a piece of plywood scrap; the cover should be 2 by 4 inches. From the plywood cut the 6⅜- by 6⅞-inch center divider.

7. Before you start the assembly, you will bore all the holes. Lay out the entrance holes by referring to the dimensions shown on the illustrations. Remember, there is an inside and an outside for the front and the back. The poorer face (the C-grade veneer) should be on the inside; the best face (the A-grade veneer) on the outside. Make sure you have the correct arrangement before cutting the entrance holes.

Wrens need a 1- to 1¼-inch entrance hole. Use a brad point or Forstner bit to drill the holes; spade bits tend to tear plywood. Use a back-up piece of scrap wood to reduce splitting when the drill bit emerges. An alternative to boring is to saw the holes. After drawing the circles with a compass, predrill a ¼-inch saw-access hole. Then carefully saw the circles with a coping saw or a scroll saw. If needed, the round side of a wood rasp can be used to shape and smooth the holes. Also drill the ¼-inch holes for the perches.

8. The chimney must have two sets of holes: two ¾-inch vent holes and two ¼-inch holes for doweling on the chimney cap. After marking the vent holes as indicated on the illustration (page 42), drill the ¾-inch holes (use a drill press if available). These go clear through the piece.

9. Mark the ¼-inch dowel holes on the chimney cap as indicated by the illustration. Clamp the cap in position on the top of the chimney, and then drill the two ¼-inch holes through the plywood cap and approximately ½ inch into the chimney.

10. Now you are ready to check the various pieces for fit. Assemble all the pieces but the roof. Make sure the smaller cleanout floor pieces fit easily in the cleanout openings cut in the bottom. Trim if necessary.

11. Using the waterproof glue and finishing nails, fasten the ends, the bottom, and the center divider. Let the glue dry thoroughly.

12. Test the roof piece to see if it is going to bend easily to the shape of the ends. If it resists, try soaking it in cold water. Don't use hot water or prolong the soaking—the plywood could delaminate. (Try soaking a test piece of scrap to ensure that the water will not harm the plywood.) To ensure a strong bond, let the soaked piece dry slightly before gluing with the waterproof glue.

You will align one end of the roof, kerfs down, against one end of the base. Apply the waterproof glue and nail the end into place. Now start the bend, wrapping the curved ends and nailing as you go. The piece should extend past the opposite end of the base. After the glue has dried, trim and sand this overhang so it is flush with the base.

Wren Apartment House

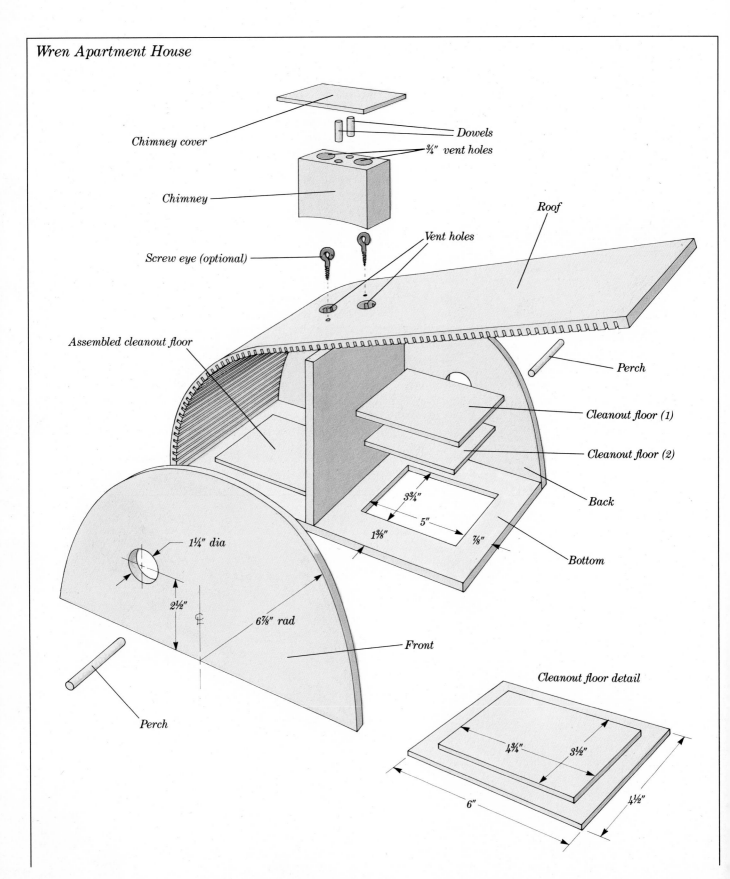

Chimney cover

Dowels

¾" vent holes

Chimney

Roof

Screw eye (optional)

Vent holes

Assembled cleanout floor

Perch

Cleanout floor (1)

Cleanout floor (2)

Back

3¾"

5"

1⅜"

⅞"

Bottom

1¼" dia

2½"

6⅞" rad

Front

Perch

Cleanout floor detail

4¾"

3½"

6"

4½"

Materials List

ACX (exterior) ¼-inch sanded plywood is the principal construction material. A piece of plywood approximately 2 by 3 feet and some miscellaneous pieces of 1 by 4 and 2 by 4 lumber should be more than necessary for all the required pieces. (See ''Building Basics,'' page 24, for discussion of materials.)

Lumber

Piece	No. of Pieces	Thickness	Width	Length
Front and back end blanks	2	¼"	7"	14"
Bottom	1	¼"	6⅜"	13¾"
Roof	1	4"	7"	23"
Cleanouts (2)	2	¼"	3½"	4¾"
Cleanout floor (2)	2	¼"	4½"	6"
Chimney cover	1	¼"	2"	4"
Center divider	1	¼"	6⅜"	6⅞"
Chimney	1	1½"	3½"	4"

Mounting block(s) or board (see discussion of mounting, page 23).
Some miscellaneous pieces of 1×4 and 2×4 lumber.

Hardware and Miscellaneous

Item	Quantity	Size	Description
Finishing nails	30 (approx.)	¾"	Galvanized or aluminum
Glue	1 small can		Waterproof
Glue	2 or 3 drops		Hot-melt
Sandpaper		80–120 grit	Medium
Finish	1 pint		Exterior primer and paint
Mounting screws	4	2" × #8	Brass, round head
Wood filler	¼ pint		
Dowels	2	¼" × 2"	For the perch
Dowels	2	¼" × 1½"	For the chimney cover

13. The cleanout floor pieces will be assembled with the smaller pieces centered on top of the larger ones; see the illustration for details. Check to see if the floors go easily up into the base and fit nicely into the holes. When you achieve the proper fit, use the waterproof glue and finishing nails to fasten the floor pieces together.

14. Now shape the base of the chimney to fit the curvature of the roof. This can be done with a drum sander, the end of a belt sander, or with the round side of a wood rasp. Keep shaping until you achieve a snug fit.

15. Place the chimney into position on the roof. With a pencil, draw the outline of the vent holes onto the roof. Remove the chimney, find the center of these two holes, and bore through the roof by using a ¾-inch bit.

16. Sand all the pieces of the wren house. Remove the ''fuzz,'' round the edges and corners, and smooth the surfaces.

17. Use the waterproof glue to fasten the chimney into its correct position on the roof. Because it is difficult to nail or screw the chimney down, the glue bond will have to suffice. Apply several coats of glue to the end grain of the chimney, and allow the glue to soak in before bonding. If possible, use some weight, a strap, or some other means to hold the chimney in place while the glue dries. After the bond is dry, make sure the vent holes are clear by poking the round side of a rasp through the chimney.

18. Attach the chimney cover by using the two ¼- by 1½-inch dowels. Flush the dowels with the top of the cap. Sand the dowels smooth after the glue is dry.

19. Use wood filler to fill in the open saw kerfs where the roof meets the ends. When the filler is dry, sand it flush with the roof. Refill any voids if necessary. On the outside of the ends, sand the area where the perches will attach. Use the waterproof glue to attach the ¼- by 2-inch dowels. Insert and give the entire project a final sanding.

20. You are almost through. Give the outside of the house a coating of exterior primer paint. When the primer is dry, finish the house with an enamel of your choice. Avoid using bright colors; some birds don't like them.

21. The Wren Apartment House should be mounted from the back, using a mounting board to permit access to the cleanouts (see ''Building Basics,'' page 23, for discussion of mounting techniques).

BLUEBIRD TREE HOUSE

The more you can make a bluebird's house look like its natural environment, the more likely you are to attract a mating couple. Bluebirds are especially sensitive to the size of the interior, the placement of the entrance, and—most important—to where you put the house. This rustic birdhouse is especially designed to attract bluebirds.

Description and Tool Requirements

This fairly simple project can be built with an attractive barky exterior (see ''Building Basics,'' page 24, for discussion of barky wood).

This bluebird house can be built with standard hand tools. Power tools, especially a radial arm or table saw, would make the project even easier. An electric drill and ¼-inch and ½-inch bits are needed. To cut the entrance hole, use an adjustable circle cutter, a 1½- or 1⅜-inch hole saw, or a large Forstner bit. If none of these is available, the hole can be cut with a hand coping saw or scroll saw.

The project can be either mounted on a post, pipe, or attached to a tree (see ''Building Basics,'' page 23, for mounting techniques).

Building Steps

1. Start the project by referring to the materials list and illustration to learn the dimensions of each piece. Saw the front, roof, and floor from the 1 by 8. Use a table or radial arm saw if available; otherwise, the pieces can be sawn with a handsaw. The front, roof, and floor require only simple square cuts. If barky slabwood is available, use it only for the front, sides, and roof.

2. The sides are cut from 2 pieces of 1 by 8, twelve inches long. Rip the 1 by 8 to a width of 5¾ inches. Lay out the slope as shown in the illustration—that is, 12 inches on one edge, 8½ inches on the other. Check the layout against the illustration before sawing. When you are sure the layout is correct, cut the sides.

3. The back should be square on the sides and bottom and have a 30-degree bevel on the top to conform with the roof pitch on the sides. Refer to the illustration to see how the back should look, then cut the back.

4. Lay out the vent holes and drainage holes as shown in the illustration. Note that if the house is to be back-mounted using a mounting board, the vent holes should be drilled in the upper rear of the sides. Drill three

Bluebird Tree House

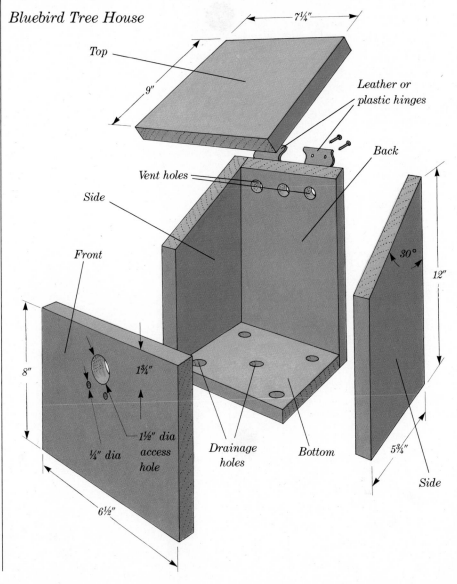

Top • 7¼" • 9" • Leather or plastic hinges • Vent holes • Back • Side • Front • 30° • 12" • 8" • 1¾" • 1½" dia access hole • ¼" dia • Drainage holes • Bottom • 5¾" • Side • 6½"

Materials List

If slabwood is used, try to find pieces ¾- to 1-inch thick. Approximately 8 lineal feet of 1 x 8 should be sufficient for this project. Rough-sawn western red cedar or redwood is an excellent wood to use for a bluebird house. Surfaced soft pine can also be used. The stock should be relatively free of large knots or other defects. (See "Building Basics," page 24, for discussion of materials.)

Lumber

Piece	No. of Pieces	Thickness	Width	Length
Front*	1	¾″	6½″	8″
Roof*	1	¾″	7¼″	9″
Bottom	1	¾″	5″	5″
Sides*	2	¾″	5¾″	12″
Back	1	¾″	5″	12″
Mounting board**	1	¾″	7¼″	16″

* Use barky slabwood if desired
**If mounting against a tree

Hardware and Miscellaneous

Item	Quantity	Size	Description
Finishing nails	24	1½″	Galvanized or aluminum
Finishing nails	30	¾″	Headed, galvanized or aluminum
Box nails	4	16d	Galvanized (for tree mount)
Hinge material	2	1″ × 6″	Leather or thick plastic
Bark	4	8″ × 12″	If not using slabwood
Pipe*	1	¾″ × 6′	Galvanized
Floor flange*	1	¾″ × 4″	Female, galvanized
Screws*	4	1″ × #8	Brass, flat head
Glue (optional)			Waterproof

* If mounted on a pipe

¾-inch vent holes in the back and two ½-inch drainage holes in the bottom. Use a piece of scrap lumber for backup to prevent splitting as the drill emerges.

5. The entrance hole should be 1½ inches in diameter. To cut this hole in the front piece, use a Forstner or spade bit; a hole saw or circle cutter can also do the job. However, if you use a circle cutter, use it in a drill press—it is dangerous to use in a hand drill.

Another alternative is to saw the entrance hole. First, predrill a ¼-inch saw-access hole, then saw the entrance hole by using a hand coping saw or scroll saw. Smooth the hole with a rat-tail or round-sided rasp.

6. Assemble all the pieces to check for squareness and fit. Correct any problems. Fasten all the parts, except the roof, by using the galvanized finishing nails; gluing is optional.

7. If you use bark on the sides, front, and roof, rough-cut the bark pieces to match the birdhouse surfaces. (See "Building Basics," page 24, for discussion of barky wood.) Tack the bark on permanently using the ¾-inch finishing nails; glue is optional. Drive the nails through the bark, into the wood. Concentrate the brads along the edges and corners.

Trim the edges of the bark to fit, using a knife or other cutting tool.

8. Using finishing nails, attach the roof to the back, using the pieces of leather or plastic as hinges.

9. If the Bluebird Tree House will be back-mounted against a tree or other object, cut and attach a mounting board to the back of the house. If the house will be post- or pipe-mounted, see "Building Basics," page 23, for mounting instructions.

Bluebirds—both Eastern and Western—favor rustic habitats. This bark-covered birdhouse is meant to approximate a tree cavity.

SCREECH-OWL BOX

Screech-owls normally like to find cavities in trees or take over abandoned nesting holes of other birds. They occasionally use birdhouses intended for flickers and Wood Ducks. Screech-owls usually lay their eggs in the rotting wood chips and rubble found at the bottom of a tree cavity. You may want to put some wood chips and bark at the bottom of this birdhouse to encourage them to nest.

Description and Tool Requirements

This basic project can be built with standard hand tools. However, a table or radial arm saw would more accurately cut the pieces, enabling you to fit them together more easily. An electric drill and a ⅛-, ⅝-, and ¾-inch bit are needed. The entrance hole should be 3 inches in diameter and is best sawn using a coping or scroll saw. Lacking these saws, use a 3-inch Forstner bit, a hole saw, or an adjustable hole cutter.

The project is best back-mounted about 15 feet high on a tree.

Building Steps

1. Refer to the materials list and the illustration for dimensions of the pieces. From the 1 by 12 saw the top and bottom, the front and back, the sides, the roof, and the mounting board. Be careful to make sure all the cuts are square to ensure a tight fit.

2. Now saw 1 inch off the 4 corners of the bottom piece, using a 45-degree cut as shown in the illustration. These make drainage holes for the box.

3. Refer to the illustration for dimensions and placement of the 3 ventilation holes in the back piece. Drill the holes, using a backup scrap to prevent splitting when the bit emerges.

Screech-owls are not nest builders, but they will use a box like this one in which to lay their eggs and shelter their young.

Materials List

Approximately 10 feet of 1 by 12 stock is needed. The wood of choice for this project is rough-sawn western red cedar or redwood. Pine or other softwoods can also be used. The lumber should be relatively free of large knots or other defects. (See "Building Basics," page 24, for discussion of materials.)

Lumber

Piece	No. of Pieces	Thickness	Width	Length
Top and bottom	2	¾"	8"	8"
Front and back	2	¾"	9½"	15"
Sides	2	¾"	8"	15"
Roof	1	¾"	9½"	10"
Mounting board	1	¾"	6"	20"

Hardware and Miscellaneous

Item	Quantity	Size	Description
Finishing nails	25	1½"	Galvanized or aluminum
Common nails	2–4	16d	Galvanized (for mounting)
Glue	¼ cup		Waterproof
Sandpaper	1 sheet	80–120 grit	Medium
Finish (optional)	1 pint		Exterior oil stain or paint
Screws	4	1½" × #6	Brass

Screech-Owl Box

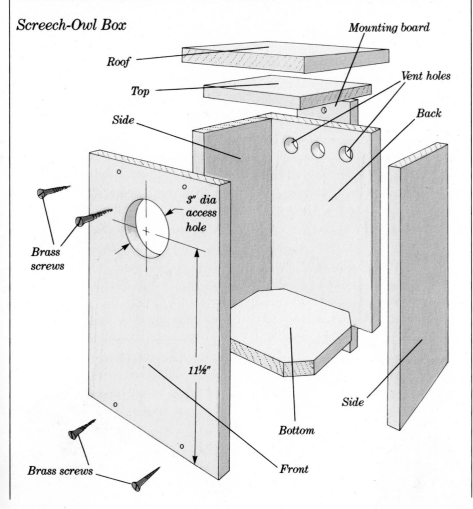

Mounting board

Roof

Top

Side

Vent holes

Back

3" dia access hole

Brass screws

11½"

Brass screws

Bottom

Front

Side

4. To drill the 3-inch entrance hole in the front, use a Forstner bit, a hole saw, or a circle cutter. (Don't forget to use the circle cutter in a drill press—it is dangerous to use in a hand-held drill.) If these tools are unavailable, sawing the hole is another option. Draw the hole on the front piece, using a compass. If sawing by hand with a coping saw or a scroll saw, predrill a saw-access hole and then cut the hole. A jigsaw can also be used for this operation if you make a plunge cut (see "Building Basics," page 22, for discussion on holes).

5. Assemble the pieces to check for squareness and fit. Make any necessary corrections.

6. Glue and nail together all the parts with finishing nails except the front. The front will be fastened by 4 brass screws, which will allow access for cleanout. Predrill the screw holes with a ⅛-inch bit to prevent splitting. When the glue is dry, sand the entire assembly to round off the corners and edges.

7. Center the mounting board on the back and attach it by using the finishing nails or screws. To prevent splitting, predrill the holes for the common nails that will attach the mounting board to the tree. It is easier to do the predrilling at your workbench than while you are on the ladder, mounting the birdhouse.

8. If you used cedar or redwood, it is perfectly acceptable to leave the box unfinished; it will weather to a soft gray. To slow the weathering, apply a finish on the outside of the box with an exterior oil stain. If paint is used, choose a dull-colored exterior enamel.

9. Mount the box on the trunk of a tree near a big bend or crotch. It should be at least 15 feet high for best results. (See "Building Basics," page 23, for mounting techniques.)

WOODPECKER HOMESTEAD

T he drumming noise of the Red-bellied Woodpecker is a welcome sound, for even if you can't see the bird, you know you have a feathered backyard visitor. This species, most common in the southeastern United States, has recently expanded its range into the Midwest and as far north as southern Ontario. Of all the woodpeckers, the Red-bellied Woodpecker is the one most likely to make use of a birdhouse, provided it is mounted at least 12 feet above the ground.

Description and Tool Requirements

This barrel-like woodpecker home can be constructed entirely with hand tools, but the use of a table saw would facilitate ripping the side pieces. The curved top and bottom are best sawn with a power jigsaw or band saw. A hole saw is used for the 2½-inch-diameter entrance hole. However, this opening can also be made with a portable jigsaw. A drill and ⁵/₃₂-inch bit are needed to predrill the screw holes.

The woodpecker residence is designed to be tree-mounted.

The Red-bellied Woodpecker is often attracted to bird-houses near suburban homes.

Materials List

Rough-sawn western red cedar is the ideal construction material for this project. Other textured softwood, preferably rough sawn, can also be used. You will need a piece of 1 by 10 or 1 by 12. Approximately 8 feet of this stock should easily do the job. The lumber should be of good grade and relatively free of large knots and other defects. (See "Building Basics," page 24, for discussion of materials.)

Lumber

Piece	No. of Pieces	Thickness	Width	Length
End blanks	2	¾"	8"	8"
Outer top blank	1	¾"	9¼"	9¼"
Side slats	14	¾"	1⁷/₁₆"	14"
Mounting board	1	¾"	1⁷/₁₆"	18"

Hardware and Miscellaneous

Item	Quantity	Size	Description
Finishing nails	70	1½"	Galvanized or aluminum
Common nails	2	12d	Galvanized
Sandpaper	1 sheet	80–120 grit	Medium
Finish	1 pint		Exterior oil stain
Screws	12	1½" × #6	Brass, round head

48

Building Steps

1. Start by cutting out the 8-inch square blanks for the two barrel ends. Then cut the 9¼-inch square outer top. Temporarily join the 2 blanks for the end pieces for gang-sawing (see "Building Basics," page 21, for techniques of duplicate cutting). Lay out a 7-inch diameter circle and, using a jigsaw or band saw with narrow blades, cut the circle. Then cut an 8½-inch-diameter circle from the blank of the outer top.

2. With the barrel-end pieces still temporarily joined, mark off 15 flat 1⁷⁄₁₆-inch edges around the circumference against which each of the side slats and the mounting board will be fastened. See the illustration for details. Use a stationary disk sander or belt sander to cut off the flats. If these tools are not available, use a wood rasp. Separate the pieces. With a pencil, mark both pieces in a way that will allow you to reunite them.

3. Now for the side slats: Rip 14 slats, using a table saw, if one is available. Then rip the mounting board.

4. Give all the parts a light sanding, removing "fuzz" and slightly rounding edges. Sand down the roughest saw marks on the outer top.

5. Two of the slats will be screwed onto the barrel ends to allow access for cleaning. To prevent the slat end from splitting, predrill the screw holes, ⅜ inch from the slat end; use a ⁵⁄₃₂-inch drill bit. Also predrill the mounting board, 2⅜ inches in from each end (see illustration).

6. Rematch the flats that you marked in step 2. Attach the mounting board first, fastening it to the 2 circular barrel ends with 1½-inch screws. The mounting board should have a 2-inch overlap beyond the ends. Using the finishing nails, fasten 2 slats to the barrel ends, one on each side of the mounting board. Use a framing square to check and adjust the slats, which should be perpendicular to the barrel ends. Use 4 finishing nails for each slat.

7. Fasten 3 more slats to each side. Check that the pieces are square. With screws, fasten the cleanout-access slats to the barrel ends (see illustration). Attach the rest of the slats with the finishing nails.

8. It may be necessary to add a thin filler slat if a gap remains in the barrel. Measure any remaining gap, and rip a 14-inch piece to fit. Fasten it into place.

9. Take the outer top, already sawn, and place it in position. A slot, ¾ inch by 1⁷⁄₁₆ inches, will have to be cut in the outer edge for the top to fit the mounting board. Mark the slot and saw it, using a jigsaw or band saw. Now, using the finishing nails, fasten the outer top into place on top of one of the barrel ends.

10. The last step is to cut the 2½-inch diameter entrance. Refer to the illustration to learn size and placement. Draw the circle with a compass. Predrill a saw-access hole. Using a hole saw or jigsaw with a narrow blade, cut the hole. Smooth it with the round side of a rasp.

11. Give the woodpecker home a final sanding, and finish the outside with an oil stain. Predrill the mounting board to prevent splitting. Using the common nails, mount the birdhouse on a tree; the house must be at least 12 feet high. See "Building Basics," page 23, for mounting techniques.

Woodpecker Homestead

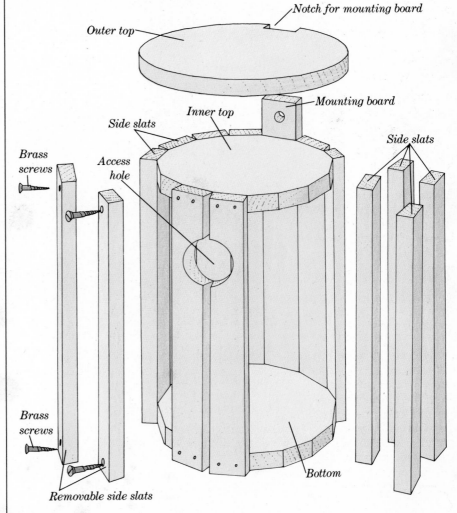

Notch for mounting board

Outer top

Mounting board

Inner top

Side slats

Side slats

Brass screws

Access hole

Brass screws

Bottom

Removable side slats

WOOD DUCK NESTING BOX

The Wood Duck was almost hunted to extinction in the earlier part of this century. It is one of the real success stories of early wildlife management. The drake Wood Duck is among the most beautiful birds in the world and today is one of the most common ducks in the eastern United States. The ideal location for this box is near wooded swamps or lake or pond borders.

Description and Tool Requirements

This project is relatively simple. Although you can do the job with hand tools, a table saw would greatly facilitate cutting—especially making the roof cuts. A band saw, coping saw, or power jigsaw, saber saw, or scroll saw are needed to saw curved roof shapes and the entrance hole. A drill and ¼-inch bit are needed to make the saw-access hole. A ⅛-inch bit is needed to predrill the screw holes. (See "Building Basics," pages 18–22, for discussion of tools and cutting techniques.)

At the start decide how the Wood Duck Nesting Box is to be mounted. It needs to be approximately 20 feet high. A common method is to nail it to a creekside tree. This solution requires a mounting board. Another option is to put it on a post. Details about preparing the mounting blocks for use with a treated 4 by 4 post appear in step 6.

To attract a pair of Wood Ducks, the nesting box should be mounted near woods and water.

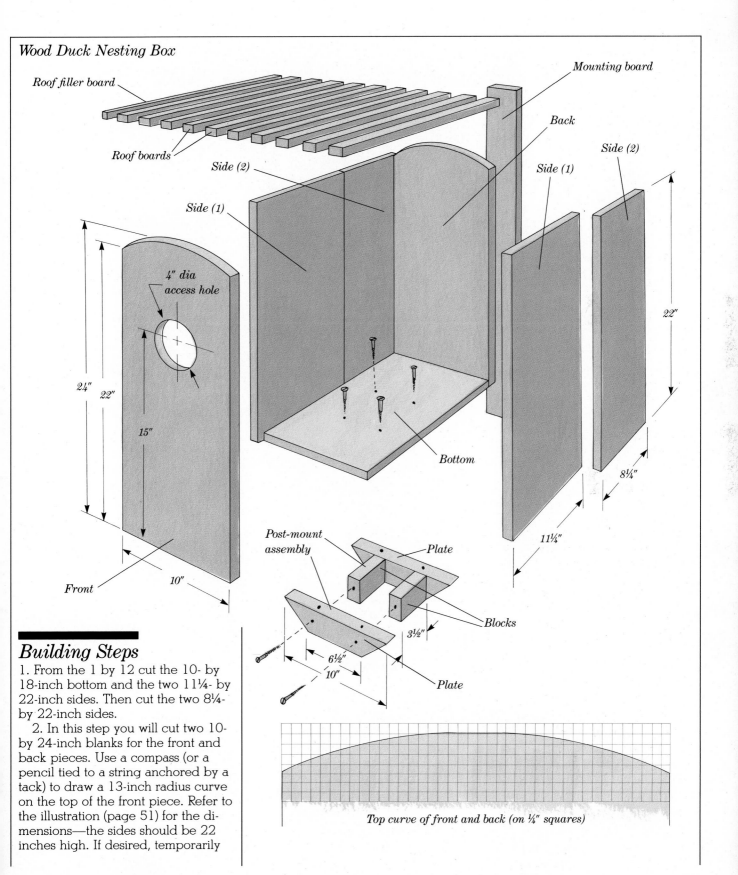

Wood Duck Nesting Box

Roof filler board

Roof boards

Mounting board

Back

Side (2)

Side (1)

Side (1)

Side (2)

4" dia
access hole

24"

22"

15"

Front

10"

Bottom

22"

8¼"

11¼"

Post-mount
assembly

Plate

Blocks

3½"

6½"

10"

Plate

Top curve of front and back (on ¼" squares)

Building Steps

1. From the 1 by 12 cut the 10- by
18-inch bottom and the two 11¼- by
22-inch sides. Then cut the two 8¼-
by 22-inch sides.

2. In this step you will cut two 10-
by 24-inch blanks for the front and
back pieces. Use a compass (or a
pencil tied to a string anchored by a
tack) to draw a 13-inch radius curve
on the top of the front piece. Refer to
the illustration (page 51) for the dimensions—the sides should be 22
inches high. If desired, temporarily

join the front and back for duplicate cutting (see ''Building Basics,'' page 21, for techniques of duplicate cutting). Use a jigsaw or band saw for making the curved cut. After sawing the front and back, sand or lightly rasp the curved edges to make them smooth. If necessary, separate the front from the back.

3. Begin creating the entrance hole by drawing a 4-inch circle on the front piece; see the illustration for hole placement. Drill a ¼-inch saw-access hole inside the circle. Using a narrow blade in the jigsaw, cut the hole. A coping saw or scroll saw can also be used. Smooth the entrance with the curved side of a rasp.

4. Now to the roof boards: Cut 10 strips, each ¼ by 21 inches; a table saw is the best tool for this. On the model shown, the roof strips are sawn square. Don't cut the roof filler board at this time.

5. If the box is to be tree-mounted, cut a 30-inch-long mounting board, 4- to 6-inches wide, depending on material available. (See ''Building Basics,'' page 23, for discussion of mounting techniques.)

6. If the nesting box is to be post-mounted, you need mounting blocks and mounting plates. The inner mounting blocks are most easily made from scraps of 2 by 4 (actual dimensions: 1½ by 3½ inches) cut 3½ inches long. Otherwise, cut from ¾-inch stock 4 pieces measuring 3½ by 4 inches. Glue the flat sides of each pair together. The mounting plates can be made from either ¾-inch or 1½-inch stock. Cut the stock with the slant shown in the illustration. (The mounting plates shown fit on a 4 by 4 post. If a different-sized post is used, adjust the block spacing.)

To prevent splitting when assembling and attaching the mounting base, predrill the holes for the 1½-inch screws (see the illustration for hole placement). Assemble the mounting base with glue and 4 of the 1½-inch screws. If 2 by 4 side plates

Materials List

Rough-sawn western red cedar is an excellent choice for this project. Redwood can also be used. Approximately 16 lineal feet of 1 by 12 is required. The stock should be relatively free of large knots and other defects. Note that the 1½-inch mounting blocks are made from face-glued ¾-inch stock (2 by 4 stock can be substituted).

Lumber

Piece	No. of Pieces	Thickness	Width	Length
Bottom	1	¾″	10″	18″
Sides (1)	2	¾″	11¼″	22″
Sides (2)	2	¾″	8¼″	22″
Front and back blanks	2	¾″	10″	24″
Roof boards	10	¾″	1¼″	21″
Mounting board**†	1	¾″	4″–6″	30″
Mounting blocks*	2	1½″	3½″	3½″
Mounting plates*	2	¾″ or 1½″	3½″	10″
Roof filler board	1	¾″	⅜″	21″

Hardware and Miscellaneous

Item	Quantity	Size	Description
Finishing nails	50	1½″	Galvanized or aluminum
Finishing nails	25	2″	Galvanized or aluminum
Glue	1 small can		Waterproof
Sandpaper		80–120 grit	Medium
Finish (optional)	1 pint		Exterior oil stain
Mounting screws*	4	2″ × #8	Brass, flat head
Mounting screws**†	4	1½″ × #8	Brass, flat head

* For post mounting
** Custom-saw to fit
† For tree or vertical surface mounting

are used, the screws should be longer. Some waterproof glues leave a purple stain, so be careful not to overapply the glue. With 4 of the 1½-inch screws, attach this assembly to the bottom of the nesting box.

7. Now assemble the sides, front, and back. Use glue and the 2-inch nails to attach the floor assembly.

8. After the assembly has dried, start attaching the roof boards to it with glue and the 1½-inch nails. Begin at each end and work toward the middle. Allow a 1½-inch overhang in the front. Make certain that the strips fit tightly against each other. In all probability a narrower strip will be required at the top. Custom-saw the roof filler board, then glue and nail it to finish the roof.

9. Give the box a light sanding, removing all the ''fuzz'' and rounding the corners and edges.

10. If the Wood Duck Nesting Box is to be tree-mounted, center the box on the mounting board. Fasten the box in place with 4 of the 1½-inch brass screws. Predrill the mounting holes at this time. Predrilling will prevent the mounting nails from splitting the wood, and the holes are easier to make in your workshop than while you are on a ladder.

11. If you used cedar or redwood, the project can be left unfinished. If a protective coat is desired, finish the outside with an exterior oil stain.

12. Mount the Wood Duck Nesting Box about 20 feet high near wooded swamps or a lake, pond, or stream.

PURPLE MARTIN CONDO

P*urple Martins are voracious eaters of mosquitoes and other flying insects. These birds are aerial feeders and need unobstructed air space in which to soar freely. Their colonies are always near a broad open area such as a field or meadow or at the edge of a lake.*

If those habitats exist near your home, you may be able to attract a small colony. To attract martins, put this house up in the spring at the first sign of their arrival. If left up all winter, starlings or House Sparrows may become unwelcome guests.

Description and Tool Requirements

The Purple Martin Condo is an assembly of eight individual birdhouses, the roofs hinged for cleanout. Because of the large number of straight and square cuts, a table saw facilitates a snug fit. Use a dado blade for notching the base. If ¼-inch cedar is used, a band saw will be needed for resawing. Access to a planer to work the stock to final size would also be useful (see ''Building Basics,'' page 20, for tips on working with thin stock). Other necessary tools include a drill with ⅛-, ¼-, and ½-inch bits and a countersink bit. Cutting the 2-inch entrance holes requires a bit, hole saw, or circle cutter of that size. As an alternative, the holes can be sawn with a coping saw, jigsaw, or scroll saw.

The base of this structure is designed for mounting on a 4 by 4 post. However, with a few design changes, the houses could be mounted on a different-sized wood post or a pipe (see ''Building Basics,'' page 23, for mounting methods).

Building Steps

1. If you plan on resawing the ¾-inch lumber to ¼ inch, start with that operation. First, rip approximately 20 lineal feet of ¾-inch stock, 6¾ inches wide. Do this on a table saw or band saw. Now mount a wide resaw blade—½ inch or wider—on the band saw. If you have a planer available, set the band saw fence to split the ¾-inch stock exactly in half (slightly less than ⅜ inch). If a planer is not available, use a band saw to

Purple Martins usually nest in colonies. If one pair makes its home in this condo, it will soon be followed by several other pairs.

create what you need; set the fence to exactly ¼ inch and make 2 passes.

Test the resaw setup with a piece of short ¾-inch stock. Check the final thickness and squareness. When the dimensions are correct, resaw all the ripped lumber. If appropriate, move to the planer and work the resawn pieces down to the final ¼-inch thickness. If a rough-sawn surface is desired, use the plane only on one face of the stock.

2. Set the ¼-inch material aside. Move to the table saw and cut the four ¾-inch-thick pieces that make up the base supports. Next, cut the 2 base pieces to size.

3. Mount a wide dado blade—½ inch or wider—in the table saw. (Your dado cutter may use more than one blade at once.) You will cut a 6-inch-wide notch, ⅜ inch deep across the center face of both base pieces. Check the illustrations (page 55); note that the base pieces are joined, notch-into-notch, to make a flush-surfaced cross. Make sure your saw will produce the notches accurately by testing the saw setup with a couple of pieces of scrap. Fine-tune the dado depth until you get the flush-surfaced fit.

4. Refer to the illustrations (page 55). Note how the base support pieces are configured to accommodate a 4 by 4 post when the house is mounted. If a different-sized post is to be used, adjust the notch locations. The notches should be ¾ inch wide by 2 inches deep. With the dado blade still in place, test the saw setup with scraps until you attain a notch-into-notch flush fit. Cut the 8 notches in the base supports, 2 notches per support.

Materials List

Western red cedar, ¼ inch thick, is the principal construction material. As noted in the previous section, it can be made by resawing ¾-inch lumber. Refer to "Building Basics," page 24, for ideas on how to obtain or make this material. Also, note that ¼-inch plywood can be substituted. In addition to the ¼-inch stock, some ¾-inch lumber is required. The stock needed for this project can come from either surfaced or rough-sawn lumber, 1 by 8 or wider. Approximately 32 lineal feet is needed. All the final pieces—both ¼ and ¾ inch—should be relatively clear, so a reasonably good grade of material is required. Use a pressure-treated 4 by 4 post for mounting.

Lumber

Piece	No. of Pieces	Thickness	Width	Length
Base	1	¾″	6″	18″
Base	1	¾″	6″	18¾″
Base supports	4	¾″	4″	20½″
Lower house fronts	4	¼″	6½″	6½″
Lower house backs	4	¼″	6″	6″
Lower house sides	8	¼″	6″	6¾″
Lower house perches	4	¼″	2″	6½″
Upper house roofs	4	¼″	6½″	9″
Upper house backs	4	¼″	6″	8″
Upper house fronts	4	¼″	6″	6½″
Upper house floors	4	¼″	6″	8″
Upper house sides	8	¼″	6″	8¼″
Mounting post	1	3½″	3½″	20′ (approx.)

Hardware and Miscellaneous

Item	Quantity	Size	Description
Finishing nails	100 (approx.)	1″	Headless
Glue	¼ cup		Waterproof
Wood filler	¼ pint		
Sandpaper		80–120 grit	Medium
Finish	1 pint		Clear exterior oil finish
Hinges	16	¼″ × ¾″	Brass, with screws
Screws	12	1½″ × #8	Brass, flat head
Wood preservative	1 pint		Brush-on type

5. Fit the base supports together, and mark the tops and bottoms of each piece. Pull them apart and trace the quarter-circle designs from the illustrations (page 55) onto each end, noting the positions of each. Saw these designs by using your coping saw or scroll saw. The pieces can be stacked in pairs, clamped, and gang-sawed (see "Building Basics," page 21, for tips on duplicate cutting).

6. Assemble and glue the base; use C-clamps to hold the 2 pieces of the base cross together while the glue dries. Clamping is also in order as you assemble and glue the base supports.

Purple Martin Condo

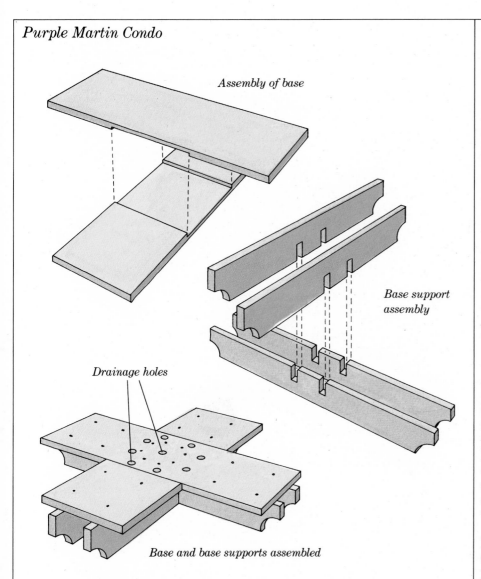

Assembly of base

Base support assembly

Drainage holes

Base and base supports assembled

Position of houses as viewed from above

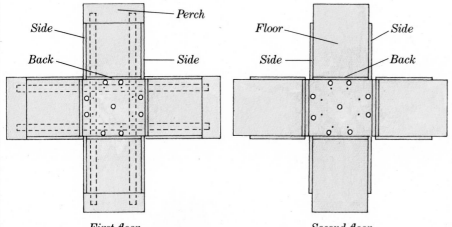

Perch

Side

Back

Side

First floor

Floor

Side

Side

Side

Back

Second floor

7. Once the glue has set on these 2 assemblies, remove the clamps. To attach the base to the base support, center the crossed base piece on the base support. Drill pilot holes down through the base and countersink them. Then glue the two assemblies together and fasten with 1½-inch brass flat head screws.

8. Now get out the ¼-inch stock. Refer to the illustration (on page 56) to learn the dimensions of the lower fronts, lower backs, lower sides, and perches. These are all square cuts; make them with the table saw.

9. Go back to the base and base support assembly. Drill ½-inch drainage holes in the center of the base cross (see the illustration at left). Stack the 4 lower backs, clamp, and gang-drill four ½-inch vent holes near the top.

Check the illustration (on page 56) to learn the position of the 2-inch entrance hole. If you are using a power saw, you may be able to stack the pieces and gang-cut the holes. A hole saw or circle cutter (in a drill press) can be used. If you prefer, the holes can be sawn using a jigsaw, coping saw, or scroll saw. First drill a saw-access hole, then insert the blade and cut. Smooth the sawn holes with the round side of a wood rasp.

10. Set the base up on your workbench. Following the illustration (page 55) carefully, set the various pieces in place, check for fit, and mark the critical locations. When all is correct, give the pieces a once-over with sandpaper to remove "fuzz" and splinters. If ¼-inch plywood is being used, fill the voids in the edges with wood filler. After the filler dries, sand it flush to the surface of the wood.

Purple Martin Condo

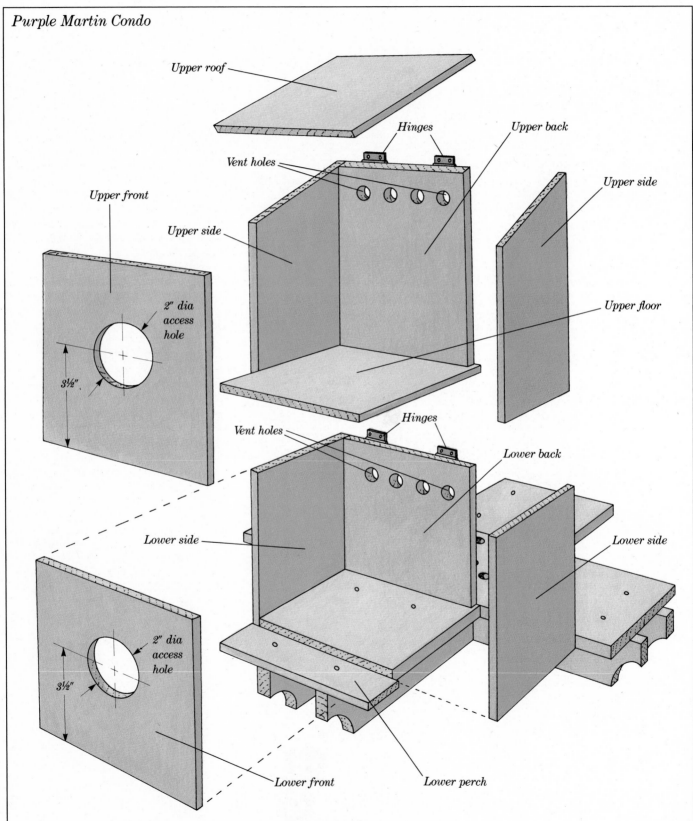

Upper roof

Hinges

Upper back

Vent holes

Upper side

Upper front

Upper side

2" dia access hole

3½"

Upper floor

Hinges

Vent holes

Lower back

Lower side

Lower side

2" dia access hole

3½"

Lower front

Lower perch

Assembly of houses

11. In this step you will start the assembly of the lower houses. Following the illustration (page 56) carefully, you will attach the sides to the backs of the 4 houses. The sides should extend ¾ inch below the back. Glue the houses into position and fasten them with 1-inch finishing nails.

12. In this step you will attach the side-back assemblies to the base. Again, study the illustration carefully—correct positioning is critical. Remember, once the glue has set, making a change will be difficult. After double-checking the illustration, glue and fasten the side-back assemblies to the base.

13. Position the perches, glue them, and use brads to fasten them into place on the base support ends, tight against the base. To complete the lower houses, use glue and brads to affix the front pieces onto the front sides of each assembly.

14. Now, back to table saw: First, from the ¼-inch stock, you will cut the upper house roofs, the upper house backs, the upper house fronts, and the upper house floors. Refer to the illustrations (page 58) for the dimensions and note that the top edge of the fronts and backs should have a 15-degree bevel to match the roof slope. Both ends of the roof piece should have this bevel, parallel to each other. After double-checking the illustrations (page 58), cut the upper house roofs, backs, fronts, and floors.

Your next task will be to saw the 8 upper house sides. Refer to the illustrations (page 58) for dimensions, and note that these pieces should slope from 8¼ to 6 inches to form a 15-degree roof pitch. Cut the upper house sides.

15. Drill the four ½-inch vent holes in the back pieces, and drill or cut the 2-inch front entrance holes.

16. Set the pieces up on the workbench and check the fit. Measure and mark pieces as necessary, checking against the illustrations. Fill any void in the edges of the plywood with wood filler. When the filler is dry, sand it flush with the surface.

17. With glue and brads, assemble the sides, fronts, and backs of the 4 upper houses. There should be a ¼-inch lip in the front and back to accept the floor pieces.

18. Attach the floor pieces with glue and brads. In 2 of the houses, the floor pieces and the backs should be flush. In the other 2 houses, the floor should extend ½ inch past the back piece. Continually check the illustration (page 59) for placement details.

19. Now, to complete the upper-house assembly, attach the roofs by using brass hinges and accompanying screws. To affix the upper house on top of the matching lower house, you will hinge the bottoms of the upper houses to the backs of the lower houses. Note in the illustrations that the 2 houses with the ½-inch bottom extensions should be opposite each other.

Fasten all the hinges onto the lower house backs. Take care that they are square. Fasten the hinges onto the upper house floors, one house at a time, getting the holes positioned and started. Remove the first 2 houses so you will have easy access to the opposite 2 houses. Then reset and attach the first houses, using a short screwdriver to drive the screws.

All 4 upper houses should tip back easily, providing access for cleaning the lower houses.

20. Give the whole assembly a final touch-up sanding. If you used cedar, apply 2 coats of an exterior oil finish on the outside of the house. You don't have to use stained oil; cedar is especially attractive with an unstained finish. Use paint for the finish if plywood was used in construction.

21. This condo is designed to be mounted on top of a 4-by-4 post. Because this post will be set in the ground, it should be pressure-treated. The post should be about 20 feet long, but remember: You are going to have to be able to reach the condo from a ladder to clean out the houses and the center opening. Place the post away from trees to help keep leaves and other debris out of the center opening.

Premount the condo on the end of the post. Drill all the mounting-screw holes. Then remove the birdhouse and set the post in the ground.

It is best to set the post in concrete. If you set a 6-inch plastic pipe into the concrete, then the post can slide in and still be taken down for maintenance. Treat both ends of the post with a brush-on wood preservative. Finally, after the concrete has dried and the post has been painted, mount the condo (see ''Building Basics,'' page 23, for discussion of mounting).

Upper and Lower House Parts

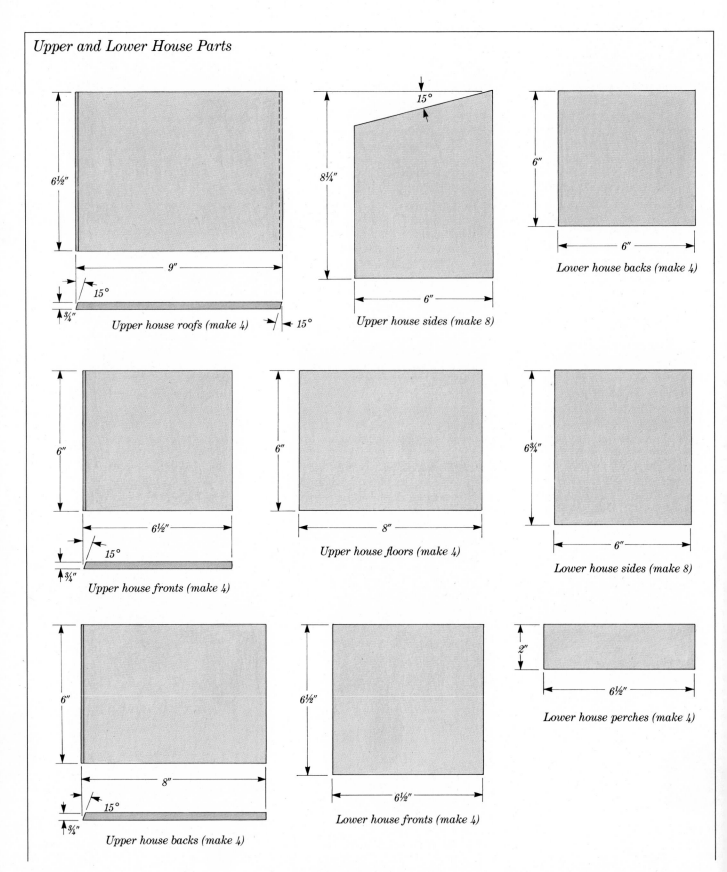

6½"
9"
15°
¾"
Upper house roofs (make 4)
15°

15°
8¼"
6"
Upper house sides (make 8)

6"
6"
Lower house backs (make 4)

6"
6½"
15°
¾"
Upper house fronts (make 4)

6"
8"
Upper house floors (make 4)

6¾"
6"
Lower house sides (make 8)

6"
8"
15°
¾"
Upper house backs (make 4)

6½"
6½"
Lower house fronts (make 4)

2"
6½"
Lower house perches (make 4)

Upper House Assembly

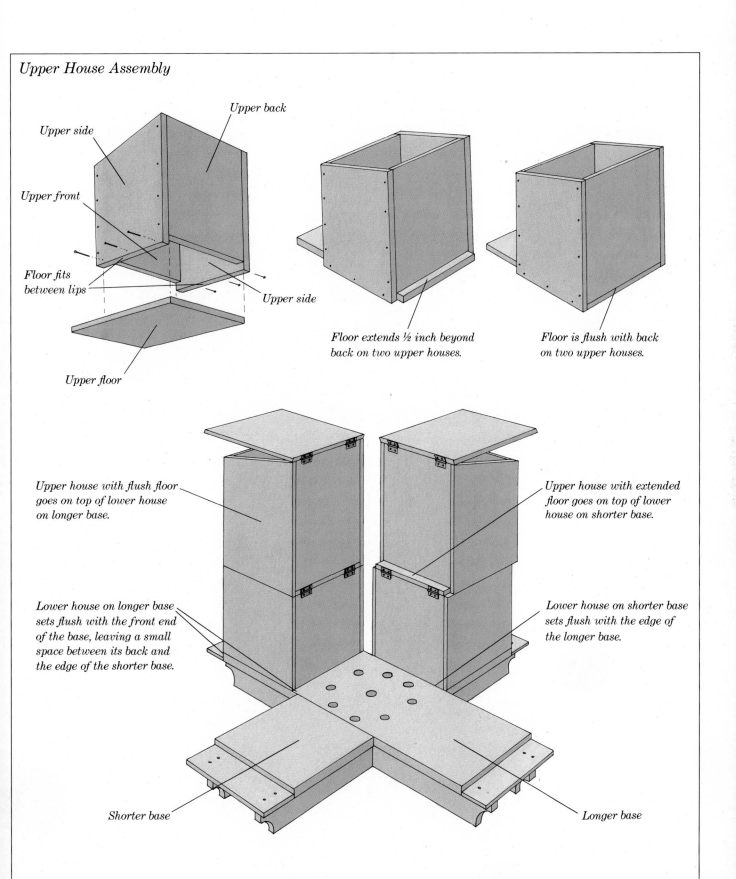

Upper side

Upper back

Upper front

Floor fits
between lips

Upper side

Upper floor

Floor extends ½ inch beyond
back on two upper houses.

Floor is flush with back
on two upper houses.

Upper house with flush floor
goes on top of lower house
on longer base.

Upper house with extended
floor goes on top of lower
house on shorter base.

Lower house on longer base
sets flush with the front end
of the base, leaving a small
space between its back and
the edge of the shorter base.

Lower house on shorter base
sets flush with the edge of
the longer base.

Shorter base

Longer base

CHICKADEE CONDOMINIUM

The Black-capped Chickadee is nonmigratory throughout its range. Some travel south of the breeding range for the winter, however, invading the home territory of the Carolina Chickadee. The two chickadees are difficult to distinguish by appearance, but their songs are somewhat different: The Carolina Chickadee's song has four notes; the Black-capped Chickadee's has two or three.

Description and Tool Requirements

This is a straightforward project that can be built with standard hand tools. Power tools, especially a radial arm or table saw, would make the project even easier. An electric drill and ⅛-, ¼-, and ½-inch bits are needed. The entrance holes require a 1⅛-inch spade bit or Forstner bit; otherwise, these holes can be made with a coping saw, scroll saw, hole saw, or an adjustable hole cutter.

The project should be mounted on a post (see "Building Basics," page 23, for mounting techniques).

Building Steps

1. You will start by cutting the square-edged chickadee house pieces from the 1 by 8. Check the illustration (page 62) and the accompanying table (page 61) for dimensions, grain direction, and angles of the bottoms, fronts, partitions, and gables. To saw the gable ends, set the miter gauge or saw arm to the angles shown in the drawing. Using a table saw or radial arm saw, if available, cut the square-edged pieces.

2. Next you will saw the side pieces and the roof parts. Both of these should have an 18-degree bevel on one edge. (This bevel cut on the side pieces is not absolutely necessary and can be cut square if only a handsaw is available.) Again, check the illustration (page 62) and Materials

Chickadees are gregarious and travel in small bands most of the year. With luck, two nesting pairs may occupy this condominium.

Materials List

Fourteen lineal feet of 1 by 8 should be sufficient for this project. Surfaced western red cedar or redwood is an excellent choice. Soft pine can also be used. The stock should be relatively free of large knots or other defects. (See "Building Basics," page 24, for discussion of materials.)

Lumber

Piece	No. of Pieces	Thickness	Width	Length
Bottoms	2	¾″	4″	8¾″
Fronts	4	¾″	5⅜″	5″
Partitions	2	¾″	4″	5¼″
Gables	4	¾″	3″	5⅜″
Sides	4	¾″	6″	8¾″
Roof (1)	1	¾″	4″	11⅛″
Roof (2)	1	¾″	4¹¹/₁₆″	11⅛″
Roof (3)	2	¾″	4¹¹/₁₆″	3″
Roof (4)	2	¾″	4″	3″
Mounting block*	2	¾″	3½″	6″
Mounting block*	1	1½″	3½″	3½″

*For mounting on a 4 × 4 post

Hardware and Miscellaneous

Item	Quantity	Size	Description
Finishing nails	50	1½″	Galvanized or aluminum
Glue	1 small can		Waterproof
Hinges	4	¾″ × 1″	Brass, with screws
Dowels, lock	4	⅛″ × 1″	
Dowels, perch	2	¼″ × 2″	
Sandpaper		80–120 grit	Medium
Caulking	1 small tube		
Finish (optional)	1 pint		Exterior oil stain
Screws	4	½″ × #6	Brass
Screw eyes	4	⅛″ holes	Brass or plated

List for details. Remember that the bevel cuts will determine the inside and outside position of these pieces. If there are any minor defects—knots, pitch seams, and so on—on one face of the wood, plan the bevel cut so it will be positioned on the inside of the house. After double-checking the layout of each piece, cut the side pieces and roof parts.

3. At this point, assemble the birdhouse pieces without glue or fasteners. First, check for fit; second, determine the best position of the parts in relation to the quality of the faces. Lightly mark each piece for final position.

4. In this step you will drill vent holes in the sides. The hole positions partially determine the final position of the pieces, so refer to the position marks you made in step 2. Use the illustrations to determine hole location. Now, using a ½-inch bit, drill 2 vent holes in each of the 4 side pieces. Use the drawings for location. Use a piece of scrap wood for backup to prevent the drill from splitting the wood when emerging.

5. Check the illustration (page 62) to learn the position of the entrance holes. Use a drill, hole saw, or hole cutter to drill the 1⅛-inch holes in the fronts. If a 1⅛-inch drill, saw, or cutter is not available, drill a saw-access hole and carefully cut the holes with a hand coping saw or a scroll saw. Smooth the holes with a rat-tail rasp. Finally, drill the ¼-inch holes for the dowel perches.

6. Now the house is ready for assembly. After rechecking the fit, glue and nail the bottoms, sides, gables, and partitions. When dry, give the assembled pieces a thorough sanding, smoothing surfaces and rounding corners and edges.

7. Attach the fronts to the bottoms by using the hinges and the hinge screws. Because the hinge screws will be going into end grain in the fronts, put a small drop of glue in each screw hole to ensure a strong fastening. The hinged fronts will enable you to clean out the houses at the end of each nesting season.

8. Using sandpaper, round the ends of four 1-inch lengths of ⅛-inch dowels. Slightly bend open the eyes of 4 small screw eyes. Slip each dowel halfway into the eyes and then bend the eyes tight around the dowel. Screw each screw eye with dowel near the bottom of each gable, about ¼ inch from the top edge of the front, until the wood dowel touches the front. When twisted vertical, they will act as a locking mechanism, keeping the fronts in place.

9. Center one chickadee house on top of the other as shown in the illustration. Make certain they are square because they will be screwed together. To be sure of the screw placement, mark the location of the sides and then the screw locations on the underside of the upper house floor. Predrill the screw holes up through the floor, using a ⅛-inch drill bit. Now, drive the 1½-inch screws down through the floor of the upper house into the sides of the lower house. The screws will hold it in place; don't use glue here.

10. Position the lower roof pieces and check them for fit. If care was used to keep the top roof in square, the roofs should fit tightly. If not, loosen the screws holding the two houses together and try to slightly

Chickadee Condominium

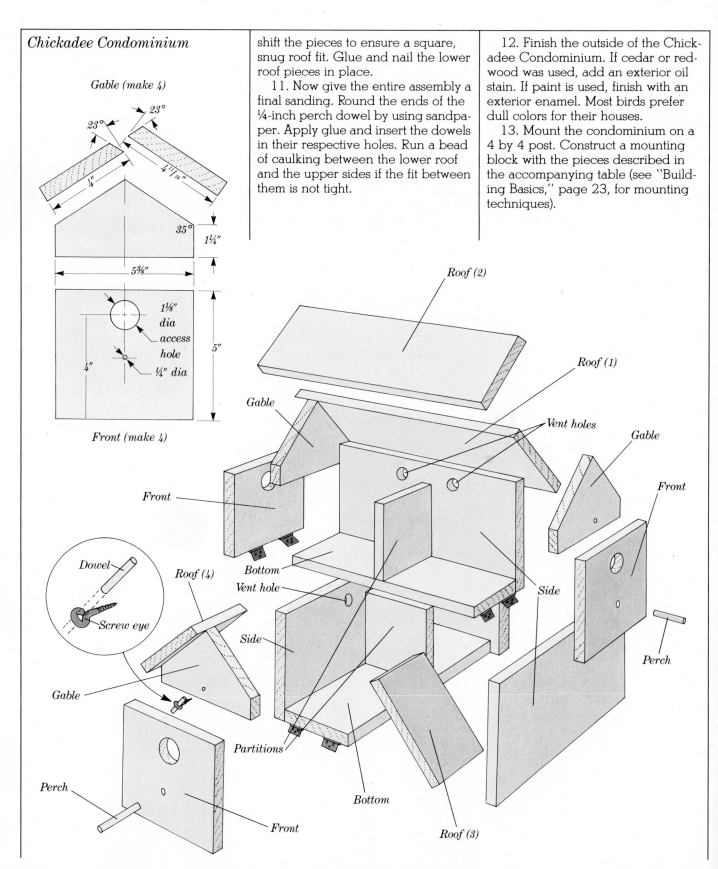

Gable (make 4)

23°

23°

23°

4"

4¹¹/₁₆"

35°

1¼"

5⅜"

1⅛" dia access hole

¼" dia

5"

4"

Front (make 4)

Dowel

Screw eye

Roof (4)

Gable

Perch

Front

shift the pieces to ensure a square, snug roof fit. Glue and nail the lower roof pieces in place.

11. Now give the entire assembly a final sanding. Round the ends of the ¼-inch perch dowel by using sandpaper. Apply glue and insert the dowels in their respective holes. Run a bead of caulking between the lower roof and the upper sides if the fit between them is not tight.

12. Finish the outside of the Chickadee Condominium. If cedar or redwood was used, add an exterior oil stain. If paint is used, finish with an exterior enamel. Most birds prefer dull colors for their houses.

13. Mount the condominium on a 4 by 4 post. Construct a mounting block with the pieces described in the accompanying table (see ''Building Basics,'' page 23, for mounting techniques).

Roof (2)

Roof (1)

Vent holes

Gable

Gable

Front

Front

Vent hole

Bottom

Side

Side

Partitions

Bottom

Roof (3)

Perch

AMERICAN KESTREL HOME

To attract North America's smallest raptor, place this nesting box at least 10 feet above ground next to an open area.

American Kestrels are the only falcons in North America that will use a birdhouse or nesting box. The birds use little or no nesting material. If you build this birdhouse, make certain it is placed 10 to 30 feet from the ground, next to an open area.

Description and Tool Requirements

In addition to the standard hand tools, this project calls for a table saw or band saw to make the beveled front pieces. A jigsaw is needed to make the curved cuts and saw the entrance hole. Also required is a drill and a ¾-inch bit, strap clamps (or rope), and 4 C-clamps. (See "Building Basics," pages 18–22, for discussion of tools and sawing techniques.)

This nesting box must be mounted up high, most likely against a tree. A mounting board is needed (see "Building Basics," page 23, for mounting methods).

Building Steps

1. Start this kestrel house by cutting the back and 2 side pieces from the 1 by 12 lumber. Use a table saw or band saw.

2. Now set the saw to cut at an 11½-degree angle. Rip the 8 front pieces so each edge has a bevel. Check the illustration (page 65) for details.

3. Cut an 8- by 9-inch piece; this is the blank from which you'll cut the bottom. Trace the final shape of the bottom from the illustration onto the blank. Saw the pattern with a band saw. Make this cut carefully, taking care not to saw inside the line.

4. Drill three ¾-inch drainage holes in the bottom piece as shown in the illustration. Note that 2 of the holes should be near the back edge.

5. Now you will check to make sure the bottom piece fits tightly with all the other pieces. Set the bottom on your workbench. Clamp the side and back pieces into place. Now temporarily assemble the beveled front pieces, by fitting them into place around the front edge of the bottom piece. Use a strap clamp around the outside of the front pieces if necessary. If the bottom prevents the front pieces from fitting tightly, sand or rasp the front of the bottom until the front edges come together snugly.

6. Give the cut pieces a light sanding, removing "fuzz" and splinters.

7. Using glue and 1½-inch finishing nails, begin the assembly. Fasten together the back, the sides, and the bottom as shown in the illustration on page 64. Note that the longer back piece should be flush with the sides at the bottom, but it protrudes ¾ inch at the top of the birdhouse.

8. Gluing the beveled front pieces comes next. Apply glue to the edges, then glue and nail the pieces to the bottom. Clamp the top and bottom together, using strap clamps or knotted ropes twisted with sticks. Drive staples into the top ends to help hold them together. Using a sponge and warm water, wash off any glue that has squeezed out from the edges.

9. Cut the 11½- by 11-inch roof blank from the 1 by 12, beveling the back edge 6 degrees. Set the blank on your workbench and turn the assembled box upside down on top of it. The house should be centered on the blank, with the back edge of the roof snug against the protruding back piece of the box. Trace the shape of the outside of the box onto the roof piece. After removing the box, draw

American Kestrel Home

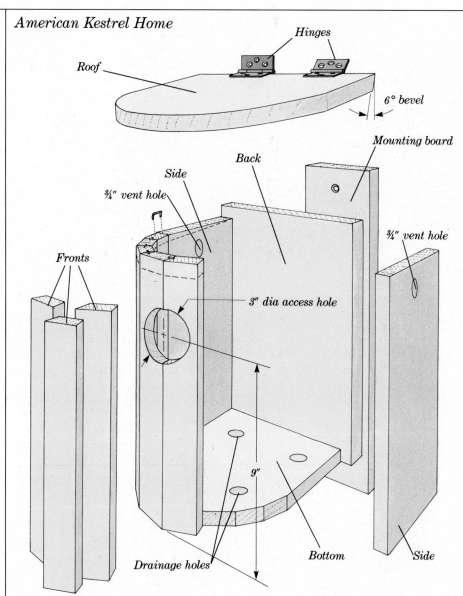

a second shape parallel to the box lines, 1 inch beyond the sides and front (see the illustration on page 65). This extra inch will provide the overhang needed for weather protection. Now, using your jigsaw or band saw, cut the roof shape.

You might want to put an overhanging lip on the roof for appearance and better weather resistance. If so, cut the roof pattern approximately ⅜ inch larger than the house instead

of 1 inch larger. Cut sections of the sides and front patterns 1 inch to 2 inches long, then glue and nail around the edges of the roof piece; trim for fit.

10. Set the box upright or on the back. Measure down 1 inch at several points in the front; draw a line connecting the points. Now, connect this line to the intersection points of the sides and back on each side of the box. This line shows the roof slope. Use a portable jigsaw to cut along the line.

Materials List

This kestrel box is built from surfaced or rough-sawn 1 by 12 western red cedar. Redwood or pine can also be used. A board 6 feet long should be sufficient for the job. The piece should be relatively free of knots. (See "Building Basics," page 24, for discussion of materials.)

Lumber

Piece	No. of Pieces	Thickness	Width	Length
Back	1	¾"	9½"	14¾"
Sides	2	¾"	5¼"	14"
Fronts	8	¾"	1¹³⁄₁₆"	14"
Bottom blank	1	¾"	8"	9"
Roof blank	1	¾"	11¼"	11"
Mounting board	1	¾"	4"–6"	18"–20"

Hardware and Miscellaneous

Item	Quantity	Size	Description
Finishing nails	40	1½"	Galvanized or aluminum
Staples	10	¾"	Galvanized
Glue	¼ cup		Waterproof
Sandpaper		80–120 grit	Medium
Finish	1 pint		Exterior oil stain or paint
Hinges	2	¾" × 1"	Brass, with screws
Screws	4	1½" × #8	Brass round head, for mounting
Screws	4	2" × #10	Brass round head, for mounting

11. Cut out the 3-inch entrance hole with the jigsaw.

12. Sand the edges of the roof smooth. Now, attach it with the hinges to the upraised back piece as shown in the illustration on page 64.

13. Attach the mounting board to the back of the kestrel box. Center the board both ways, and predrill holes for the mounting screws. Attach the board by using the 1½-inch screws.

14. Give the home a final sanding. If you used cedar or redwood, an oil stain on the outside will provide weather protection and will look attractive. If you used pine, finish the home with a dull-colored exterior enamel paint.

15. The American Kestrel Home should be mounted 10 to 30 feet high and against a tree near an open area or field. Use the 2-inch screws to fasten the mounting board (see "Building Basics," page 23, for mounting techniques).

American Kestrel Home

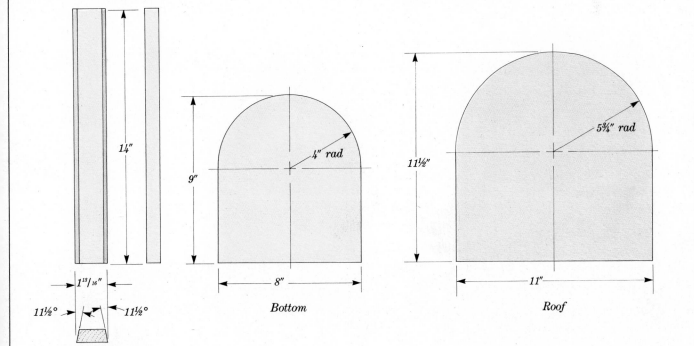

Fronts (make 8)

Bottom

Roof

CONSTRUCTING BIRD FEEDERS

Feeding birds is one of the most popular hobbies in the United States. More than 60 million people are involved in backyard bird feeding for at least part of the year. A bird feeder will attract many different species of birds. Birds that winter in your region will be most appreciative of the food left out for them. So, too, the birds of summer will take advantage of well-stocked feeders. You can enjoy a variety of feathered backyard visitors the year around by building one or more of the 12 attractive bird feeders described in this book. The feeder designs were created not with just the aim of attracting birds; they also will be handsome additions to your backyard habitat.

Bird feeders can be decorative or whimsical, but they also must be functional. They need the capacity to contain and dispense seed and a platform upon which the birds can alight.

LIGHTHOUSE BIRD FEEDER

T*his will be a beacon that points the way to food for your backyard feathered friends. This feeder will hold quite a bit of seed. Its windows allow you to see the food level and tell when it's time for refilling.*

Description and Tool Requirements

A table saw is required to build this project. Building the Lighthouse Bird Feeder also requires a power jigsaw or band saw, a drill, and standard hand tools. Bits required include a ⅛-inch bit and a 1¾-inch bit. In addition, you need a hole saw or circle cutter. A coping saw or scroll saw is needed for window construction, and so is a router with a ¼-inch rabbeting bit. Some strap clamps or rope and a couple of small C-clamps are also necessary.

The Lighthouse Bird Feeder is a tapered 12-sided polygon made up of tapered and beveled side pieces. You will need a taper jig for your table saw.

The feeder can be mounted only from the base, so it lends itself to a post- or pipe-mount. Refer to the discussion on mounting in "Building Basics," page 23.

The Lighthouse Bird Feeder will provide a nautical touch to the garden.

68

Building Steps

1. The first step is to saw the strip edging while you still have the long length of lumber. Select a clean, un-marred edge with straight grain (rip the edge smooth if necessary). Use the table saw and your smoothest-cutting blade to rip a ⅛-inch strip. Cut the strip a little longer than 44 inches. Recheck to make sure the grain is straight. Test-bend the strip into a circle to make sure it is not going to break. If necessary, cut another strip that can pass the test.

2. Each 14-inch side piece should have a 15-degree bevel on both edges. The pieces taper from 1⅝ inches at one end to 1⅜ inches at the other; the total taper is ¼ inch, ⅛ inch on each side. Take care in tapering. Remember, you are working very close to a moving saw blade, which can saw fingers even more easily than wood. Use a push stick to guide the pieces past the whirling saw blade. Hold the taper jig and the side pieces firmly down on the table.

First square-saw 12 side pieces, 1¾ by 14 inches. Cut a couple of extras to be used in setup. Now, set your taper jig so it tapers ⅛ inch in 14 inches. It might take a couple of practice cuts to achieve this. Now crank your saw blade to a 14-degree tilt. Adjust your fence so that the saw cut starts just on the end of the piece. Rip down one side of all the pieces.

Next, readjust the taper jig so it tapers ¼ inch in 14 inches. Reset the

Materials List

Surfaced soft pine (Ponderosa, white, or sugar) is ideal for this project. Certainly, other woods—including hardwoods—can be used. Use 1 by 6 or 1 by 8 stock. Five feet of stock should more than be enough. The lumber should be of good grade and relatively free of large knots and other defects. In addition, you need a 14-inch square of ⅜- or ½-inch ACX (exterior) plywood (or hardwood of the same size), several pieces of ¼-inch ACX plywood (or hardboard of the same size), and a short length of 2 by 4. (See "Building Basics," page 24, for discussion of materials.)

Lumber

Piece	No. of Pieces	Thickness	Width	Length
Strip edging	1	⅛"	1"	44"
Side blanks	12	¾"	1⅝"	14"
Lid blank	1	¼" plywood	6"	6"
Inside lid blank	1	¾"	4"	4"
Lid cap blank	2	¾"	4"	4"
Spacer mounting block	1	1½"	3½"	3½"
Side blocks	2	¾"	3½"	6"
Feeder base	1	⅜" plywood	14"	14"
Window rings	3	¼" plywood	2"	2"

Hardware and Miscellaneous

Item	Quantity	Size	Description
Wood ball	1	1½" dia.	
Clear plastic	3	⅛"	Round, 2¼" dia.
Glue	1 small can		Waterproof
Sandpaper	2 sheets	100–150 grit	Medium and fine
Finish	1 pint		Exterior paint
Screws	4	2" × #8	Brass, flat head
Screws	4	1¼" × #6	Brass, flat head
Dowel	1	¼" × 3⅛"	
Finishing nails	12	¾"	Headed, galvanized or aluminum

fence so that the large end of the piece will be exactly 1⅝ inches wide (see illustration on page 71). Practice ripping a test piece to see if the setting is correct. If all is fine, rip the remaining sides.

3. Test-fit the pieces. Make any corrections needed for a snug fit. Then saw ⅝ inch off the wide ends of 4 of the side pieces. These will become the feed openings at the base when the lighthouse is assembled. This cut should be square with the centerline of the pieces, so the miter gauge should be set a couple of points off 90 degrees.

4. Glue and assemble the tapered 12-sided polygon, being careful to place the 4 shorter pieces opposite each other, as the illustration (page 70) shows. The pieces should be flush with the other sides at the small, or top, end.

Use web or strap clamps to hold both ends while the glue dries. If these clamps are unavailable, use a knotted rope tightened with a stick.

5. Go back to the table saw and cut the blanks for the lid, inside lid, and lid caps. If the feeder is going to be mounted on a wood post, cut the mounting spacer block and the two side blocks.

6. Align and face-glue the two pieces of the lid cap to make one piece 1½ inches thick. Use C-clamps to hold them together.

7. While the glue on the lid cap is drying, you will cut the feeder base. Lay out a circle 14 inches in diameter on the ⅜- or ½-inch plywood. Use a compass (or a pencil tied to a string

Lighthouse Bird Feeder

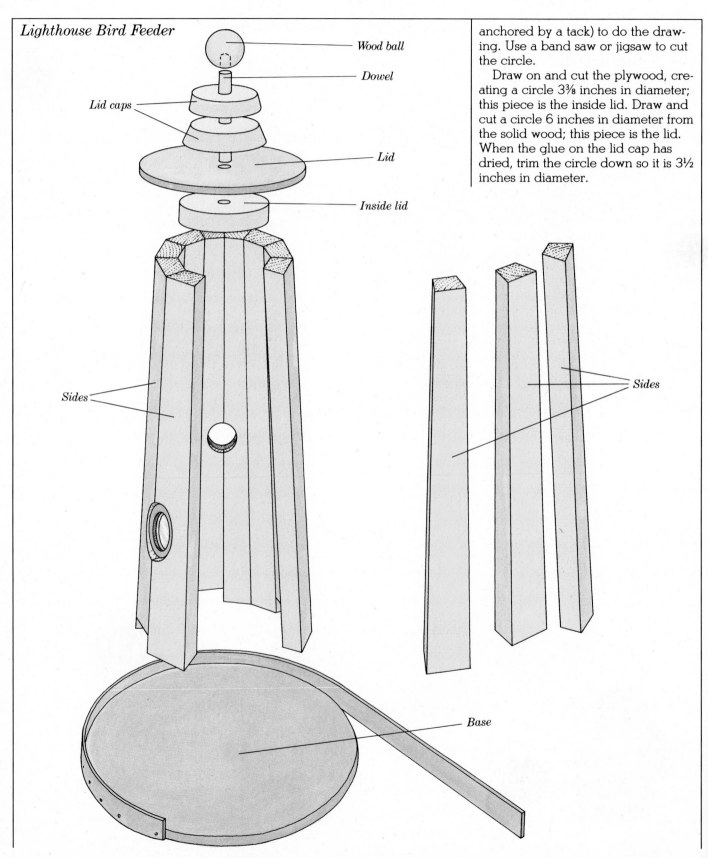

Wood ball

Dowel

Lid caps

Lid

Inside lid

Sides

Sides

Base

anchored by a tack) to do the drawing. Use a band saw or jigsaw to cut the circle.

Draw on and cut the plywood, creating a circle 3⅜ inches in diameter; this piece is the inside lid. Draw and cut a circle 6 inches in diameter from the solid wood; this piece is the lid. When the glue on the lid cap has dried, trim the circle down so it is 3½ inches in diameter.

8. Drill a ¼-inch hole halfway into the 1½-inch wood ball, being careful to keep the hole centered. Drill ¼-inch holes all the way through the three lid parts. Apply glue, then drive the ¼-inch dowel through these parts and into the ball, to hold them together. After the glue dries, sand off any extra dowel so the dowel end is flush with the bottom of the inside lid. Check the illustration (page 70) for the details.

9. The next job is tricky: You will bore three 1¾-inch holes through the lighthouse body. You have already put a lot of work into the body assembly, so you don't want to damage it at this point. Mark the window locations. To cut the holes, use a 1¾-inch Forstner bit, spade bit, or hole saw. If you don't have these tools, use a circle cutter. If possible, use the circle cutter in a drill press; a circle cutter can be dangerous in a hand drill. Whatever tool you use, take care that the holes are square with the sides of the lighthouse body.

10. This is another tricky operation, so take care. With a router and a ¼-inch rabbet bit, cut a lip ¼ inch deep around the outside edge of the window openings. If a router or rabbet bit are not available, the lip can be hand-cut by using a small chisel or carving knives.

11. There is one more sawing job, the cutting of the three window rings from the ¼-inch plywood or hardboard. Start by laying out the rings on the plywood. The outside diameter is 2¼ inches, the inside is 1¾ inches. With the tool you used to cut out the window openings, drill the inside circles. Now saw the outside of the rings by using a jigsaw, coping saw, scroll saw, or band saw. Check and adjust the size so they fit snugly into the window openings.

12. Now is the time to give all the pieces a good sanding. Use wood filler to fill any voids in the plywood lid edges or any other imperfections in the feeder parts. Start with medium-grit sandpaper to remove excess filler, saw marks, and the like. Then use fine-grit paper to achieve a smooth finish. Use any available sanding equipment for this job.

13. In this step you will center and attach the base to the bottom of the lighthouse. A good way to ensure alignment is to trace the outline of the lighthouse bottom on the bottom of the base. Then drill four ⅛-inch pilot holes for the screws through the bottom of the base into the bottom of the house. Countersink the screw holes so the flat-head screws will be flush with the wood surface. Attach the base to the bottom by using the 1¼-inch screws.

If the lighthouse feeder is to be mounted on a wooden post, the spacer block needs to be attached to the center of the bottom of the base. Using a slightly larger drill bit than before, drill 4 pilot holes. Use glue and the four 2-inch screws to attach the spacer block.

14. Use glue and finishing nails to attach the ⅛- by ¾-inch edging strip around the perimeter of the base to form a ledge. For a tight fit trim the end where the two join. This strip will help keep the birdseed from falling to the ground.

15. After a final light sanding, give the exterior of the lighthouse feeder several coats of paint. You may want to paint the still unused window rings a contrasting color.

16. Now cut the clear plastic to make three circular windows, each 2¼ inches in diameter. Apply glue to one window ring. Place one plastic window into position. Install the glued window ring to hold the window in position. Position the other windows in the same way.

17. Post-mount or pipe-mount the feeder (see "Building Basics," page 23, for details).

Lighthouse Bird Feeder

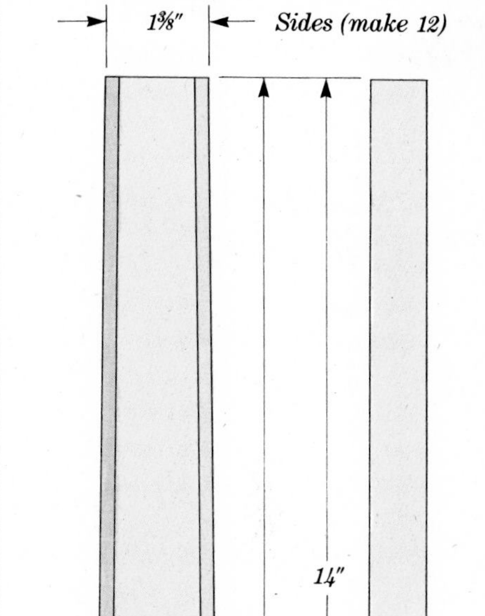
1⅝"
Sides (make 12)
14"
13⅜" *
1⅝"
¾"
15°
15°
*Cut ⅝" off 4 sides for feed openings

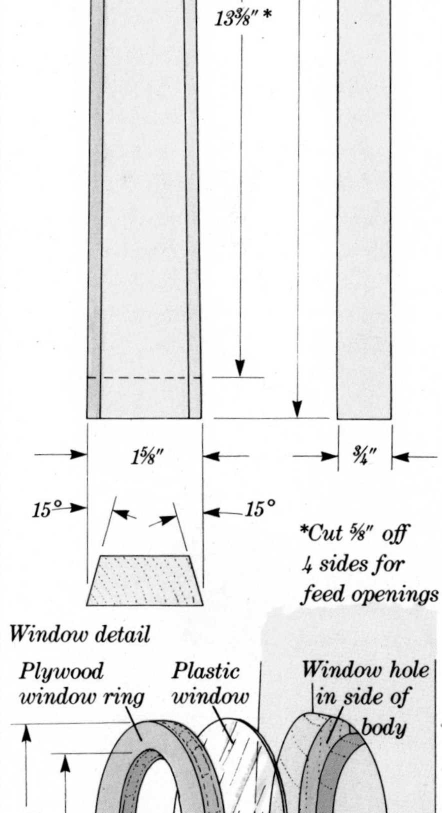
Window detail
Plywood window ring
Plastic window
Window hole in side of body
2¼"
1¾"
Rabbet

HUMMINGBIRD FEEDER

Once you hang this hummingbird feeder in your backyard, you can probably attract at least one of the species common to your part of the country. Most hummingbirds are quite territorial and will fight to keep other birds away from a food source. Ruby-throated Hummingbirds, common to the eastern United States, have been known to attack and drive off birds as large as hawks.

Description and Tool Requirements

This project is reasonably simple and can be built with basic hand tools. It requires a jigsaw or band saw to cut the inside and outside circles; a coping saw or scroll saw can be used instead. A drill and a ¼-inch bit is needed to start the inside cuts. A drum sander would be useful for final smoothing of the inside circles. Several clamps with 5- or 6-inch openings are also needed. Refer to "Building Basics," pages 18 to 22, for discussions of tools, techniques, and holes.

Building Steps

1. Using a drawing compass draw the circles, inside and outside, on the 2 by 6 stock. The outside circle should be 4¼ inches in diameter, the inside circle should be 3¾ inches.

2. Saw the outside circles, using a jigsaw, band saw, or coping saw. Use a narrow, fine-cut blade. The inside circles can be sawn with the band saw, but you must glue the entrance cuts shut when finished. If you prefer not to do this, drill ¼-inch saw-access holes inside the circles, and cut them out with a jigsaw, coping saw, or scroll saw. Tend toward undersizing the inside circles as you saw them.

The inside circles need to fit snugly around the plastic bottle. A drum sander is an excellent tool with which to do the final fitting and smoothing

Materials List

Western red cedar or redwood works well for this project, but any 2 by 6 material on hand will work. Approximately 18 inches of knot-free material is needed.

Lumber

Piece	No. of Pieces	Thickness	Width	Length
Circles	3	1½"	5½"	5"

Hardware and Miscellaneous

Item	Quantity	Size	Description
Glue	1 small can		Waterproof
Sandpaper		80–120 grit	Medium
Finish	1 pint		Exterior paint
Eye bolt	1	¼" × 2½"	Plated, with 2 nuts and washers
Silicone glue	1 tube		
Plastic tubing	4	¼" × ¾"	
Plastic bottle	1	3¾" × 7"	1 quart size with wide top

Once a hummingbird finds the feeder, it will be a regular visitor.

of the inside edges. Check the fit of the bottle as you do this.

3. Align the 3 rings on top of each other and glue them with waterproof glue. Use clamps and wood pads for this assembly. After the glue has dried, sand the outside. Use a belt sander if available.

4. Drill a ¼-inch hole in the center of the plastic bottle. With one nut and washer in place, insert the eye bolt in the hole; place the second washer and screw on the second nut. The plastic should be sandwiched between the two washers and nuts as shown in the illustration. You may have to use pliers or some other device to get the inside washer and nut in place inside the plastic bottle. Before final tightening, seal around the hardware with the silicone glue.

5. Now, liberally apply the silicone glue to the inside of the rings, and slip them over the top of the plastic bottle. Position as shown in the illustrations. Wipe off any excess glue before it sets.

6. The eye bolt is, of course, the top of the feeder. Drill four ¼-inch holes through the wood rings and plastic bottle, sloping upward. Again, check the illustration for the correct position.

7. Give the holes a good shot of the silicone glue, then insert the 4 pieces of plastic tubing into the holes. Make sure they penetrate the plastic bottle. Clean out any excess glue from the insides of the tubes before it sets.

8. Give the wood a final sanding, rounding the edges. You will probably want to paint the feeder; the classic color to attract hummingbirds is bright red. You may also want to paint some brightly colored flower petals around the feeding tube.

9. The feeder can be hung from the eaves, a branch, or some other convenient place. Hang it low enough so it can be easily removed and refilled.

Hummingbird Feeder

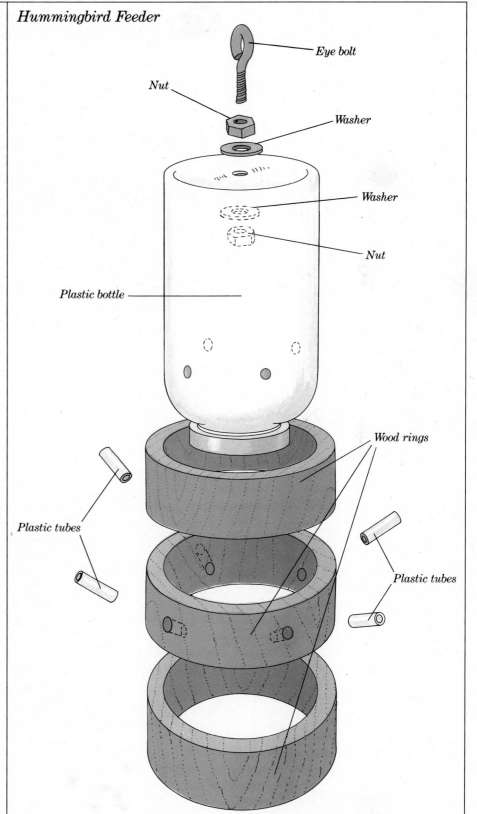

Eye bolt

Nut

Washer

Washer

Nut

Plastic bottle

Wood rings

Plastic tubes

Plastic tubes

SUET FEEDER

This suet feeder is an easy weekend project. You may want to make several. Because squirrels, raccoons, and house cats also like suet, make certain you place this feeder where they can't reach it.

Description and Tool Requirements

This is a very basic project that can easily be built with standard hand tools. If available, a table or radial arm saw would make cutting more accurate.

You have the choice of using stiff hardware cloth (wire netting) or plastic netting (the kind that is often used for bagging potatoes and onions) for the suet holders, or cages. Tin snips are needed to cut the hardware cloth; scissors can cut the plastic netting. A staple gun would be handy to attach either type of holder to the nailers.

The suet feeder can be either hung or post-mounted (see "Building Basics," page 23, for discussion of mounting techniques).

Building Steps

1. Cut a piece of 4 by 4 for the center block. If there is no short piece of 4 by 4 around, cut two 6-inch pieces of 2 by 4 and use common nails or glue to fasten them together (use waterproof glue). Cut the 4 nailers from ¾-inch stock. The base can come from a scrap piece of 1 by 10 or 1 by 12, plywood, board, or whatever you have handy. If it is plywood or board, make sure it is exterior grade.

2. Next, nail the nailer pieces onto the 4 sides of the center block, using the finishing nails. Don't attach the block to the base at this time.

In the winter, feeders offering suet will attract a variety of insect-eating birds needing an easy source of high-energy food.

Materials List

Almost any wood scraps in your shop can be used to build this very basic project. Cedar or redwood is preferred, but any other wood is satisfactory. The center block can come from a short piece of 4 by 4 or be made from 2 pieces of 2 by 4 nailed or glued together. The base can come from a short piece of 1 by 10 or 1 by 12 or a scrap piece of exterior board or plywood.

Lumber

Piece	No. of Pieces	Thickness	Width	Length
Center block	1	3½"	3½"	6"
Nailers	4	¾"	3½"	6"
Base ·	1	½"–¾"	12"(approx.)	12"(approx.)

Hardware and Miscellaneous

Item	Quantity	Size	Description
Finishing nails	16	1½"	Galvanized or aluminum
Common nails	8	8d	Galvanized
Glue	2-tube set		Epoxy
Finish	1 pint		Exterior oil stain or paint
Hardware cloth or	4 pieces	6" × 9½"	¼" galvanized
plastic netting	4 pieces	8" × 9½"	¼" netting
Staples	50	½" or ⅝"	Aluminum
Screw eye	1	¼"	Brass, galvanized or plated
Sandpaper	1 sheet	80–120 grit	Medium

Suet Feeder

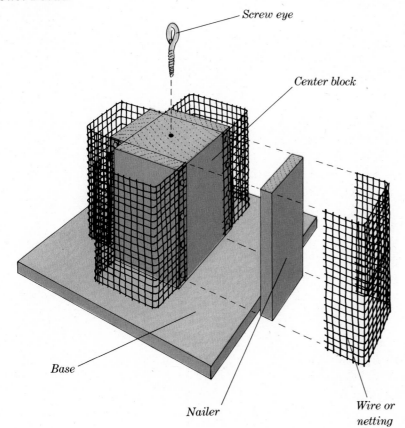

Screw eye

Center block

Base

Nailer

Wire or netting

3. Give the parts a light sanding to remove "fuzz" and slightly round the edges. Apply oil stain or paint to the outside of all the pieces. Be sure the end grain of the center block assembly gets a good coating for weather protection.

4. If you have elected to make the suet baskets from hardware cloth, cut the 4 pieces, using tin snips. Cut it carefully, close along parallel strands, to prevent sharp wire ends from sticking up. Smooth the cut edges with a file, bench grinder, or sander. Bend the pieces over a piece of wood and, with a hammer, form them into a U-shape, making the sides 3 inches and the front 3½ inches.

If using plastic netting, use scissors to cut pieces from the potato or onion bag. Cut the pieces somewhat oversize—they can be trimmed later.

5. In this step you will attach the hardware cloth baskets or the plastic netting to the center block as shown in the illustration (page 75). Staple the basket or netting to the sides of the 4 nailers. If the wire basket seems as if it might pull out the staples, reinforce them with a few more staples. If using plastic netting, draw the bottom up and staple it to the bottom of the nailers. Tap the staples down with a hammer to make sure they are tight. Trim any excess plastic netting.

6. In this step you will place the center block upside down and attach the base. Drive the galvanized common nails into the base from the bottom. Twist the screw eye into the center of the top of the block. Because the eye is embedded in end grain, place some epoxy glue around the stem of the screw eye to give it additional strength. Hang the feeder with galvanized wire or plastic rope.

CAROUSEL BIRD FEEDER

T his feeder is de-
signed to hold four
different kinds of
birdseed. The unusual de-
sign can add a light-
hearted air to the garden
decor. It will be the birds
very own backyard
merry-go-round and is
certain to have a lot of
visitors.

Description and Tool Requirements

In addition to standard hand tools, this project calls for a band saw, jigsaw, or saber saw. A table saw or band saw is needed to rip the inside barrel staves. To cut out the horse openings, a hand coping saw or a scroll saw is required. A drill with ¼-, ¾-, and 1-inch drill bits is also needed. (See "Building Basics," page 18, for discussion of tools.)

This feeder is designed to be base-mounted on a deck or on a wood or pipe post. It can be hung from the base also. In the design that follows, parts for a pipe mount are specified. (See details on mounting in "Building Basics," page 23.)

Building Steps

1. Your first task will be to cut 5 blanks from the ¼-inch plywood. These blanks will eventually become the outside circles of the feeder. Cut one 23-inch blank, two 17-inch blanks, and two 11-inch blanks.

Using a compass (or a pencil tied to a piece of string anchored by a tack), on the 23-inch blank draw a circle with a 22-inch diameter. Install a fine-cut blade in a band saw, jigsaw, or coping saw. (A hand coping saw can be used if a power saw is not available.) Cut the 22-inch circle, which is the base of the piece.

Using the same method, draw a 16-inch circle on one 17-inch blank. Temporarily join the two 17-inch

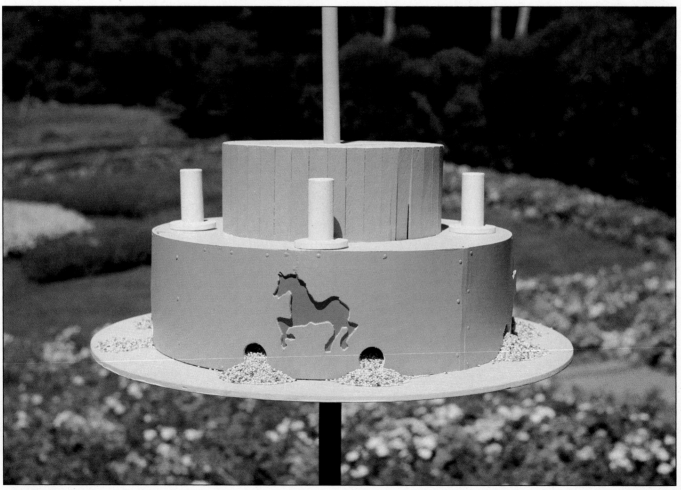

Youngsters in the home should enjoy seeing a variety of birds feeding on the Carousel Bird Feeder.

blanks, faces together, for gang-sawing (see "Building Basics," page 21, for discussion of duplicate cutting). Cut the 16-inch circles, which are outer rings, top and bottom.

In the same fashion, draw a 10-inch circle on one 11-inch blank, temporarily join the two 11-inch blanks, and cut the circles. These circles are the inner barrel, both top and bottom.

2. Now draw the smaller 10-inch circle inside the 16-inch outer ring top. Use the same center point you used in step 1. Drill a ¼-inch saw-access hole inside the penciled circle. Then cut on the marked line to create a ring. A jigsaw or saber saw is the best tool for making this cut, although a coping saw or scroll saw can be used.

3. Move to the table saw. Saw the 2 exterior wall pieces from the ⅛-inch plywood; see the illustration for dimensions (page 79). Use a plywood or fine-cut saw blade to prevent splitting the edges. Note: You might want to saw these pieces slightly longer than the dimensions given; then after fitting, cut them to the final length.

4. From ¾-inch stock you will rip 41 pieces to create the ⅛-inch-thick inner wall slats, or staves. You might want to cut the ¾-inch stock to double length—that is, 18¼ inches long—then rip the ⅛-inch slats, and finally crosscut them to the specified 9-inch length. Be sure to use a push stick and a hold-down while ripping these thin pieces. (See "Building Basics," page 20, for discussion of sawing techniques.)

5. Finish up on the table saw by cutting the 4 inside dividers from the ¾-inch stock and the 4 collar blanks from the ¼-inch plywood. They are square-cut at this time.

6. Drill four 1-inch holes in the outer ring top as shown in the illustrations (page 79). Before drilling the collar blanks, find the center point and, with a compass draw a 2-inch-diameter circle on each. Drill four 1-inch holes, one in the center of each collar blank.

Drill eight 1-inch holes near the lower edge of the ⅛-inch exterior wall pieces; the holes should be centered ¾ inch from the edge. The placement of these holes is important, so be sure to check the illustrations (pages 78 and 79). Finally, drill a ¾-inch hole in the center of the inner top and bottom. To prevent the wood from splitting when the drill emerges, use a piece of scrap lumber under all the pieces being drilled.

7. There are still a few sawing jobs; these call for a coping or scroll saw using a very fine-cut blade. Cut along the line drawn on the collar blank to make a circle 2 inches in diameter.

8. Your next job is to trace the outline of the prancing horses in the appropriate locations on the ⅛-inch plywood exterior wall pieces. One way to do this is to use carbon paper to copy the horse outline onto a piece of thin cardboard. Carefully cut the outline on the cardboard, with scissors or a craft knife. Then trace the outline onto the plywood.

Now, drill a ¼-inch saw-access hole inside each horse outline on the ⅛-inch plywood. Carefully saw the piece with your coping saw or scroll saw.

Materials List

The principal construction material is ACX (exterior) ¼-inch plywood. A piece approximately 2 by 6 feet should be ample. A piece of ⅛-inch ACX plywood, 1 by 3 feet, is needed for outside walls. Finally, a 1 by 6 piece of cedar, redwood, or pine, 4 feet long, is also required. (See "Building Basics," page 24, for discussion of materials.)

Lumber

Piece	No. of Pieces	Thickness	Width	Length
Circular base blank	1	¼"	23"	23"
Outer ring top and bottom blank	2	¼"	17"	17"
Inner ring top and bottom blank	2	¼"	11"	11"
Exterior walls	2	⅛"	5"	26⅛"
Inner wall slats	41	⅛"	¾"	9"
Inside dividers	4	¾"	3"	5"
Collar blanks	4	¼"	2½"	2½"

Hardware and Miscellaneous

Item	Quantity	Size	Description
Finishing nails	40	½"	Galvanized or aluminum
Finishing nails	90	¾"	Headed, galvanized or aluminum
Glue	1 small can		Waterproof
Glue	2-tube set		Epoxy or silicone
Abrasive paper		80–120 grit	Medium
Wood filler	¼ pint		
Finish	1 pint		Exterior primer and paint
Dowels	1	¾" × 18"	For the flagpole
Dowels	4	1" × 3"	For the plugs
Plastic	4	5" × 6"	.040" gauge, bright orange
Mounting screws	6	1" × #8	Brass or galvanized, flat head
Iron pipe	1	¾" × 6'	Galvanized, threaded one end
Floor flange	1	¾" female	Galvanized

Carousel Bird Feeder

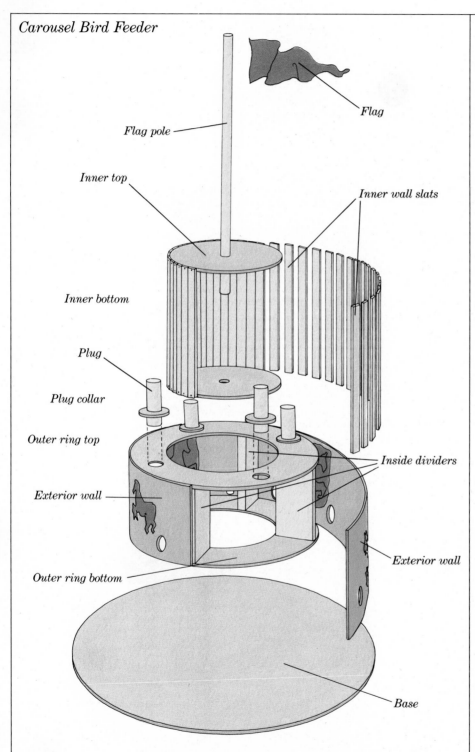

Flag

Flag pole

Inner top

Inner wall slats

Inner bottom

Plug

Plug collar

Outer ring top

Inside dividers

Exterior wall

Exterior wall

Outer ring bottom

Base

11. You will begin the assembly by gluing and tacking the ⅛-inch by 9-inch slats tightly around the 2 plywood inner circles to form a barrel, or drum. Use the waterproof glue and the ½-inch finishing nails. Check occasionally with a framing square as you go, to make sure the pieces are perpendicular to the inner top and bottom circle; a tight barrel will be the result. If a narrow gap is left where the pieces should meet, fill the gap with a narrower slat or wood filler. After the filler dries, sand it flush to the wood surface.

12. Using the waterproof glue, attach the 4 divider boards to the outer bottom, carefully aligning them flush with the edges. Check the illustrations for placement (page 78). Use the ¾-inch finishing nails to fasten the divider boards into position. Use the waterproof glue again to attach the top outer ring around the top of the divider board assembly. Tack the outer ring into position with the ¾-inch nails. Using the same glue and fasteners, attach the inner barrel, made in the previous step, into the center of this assembly.

13. Fasten this assembly to the circular base by using the waterproof glue and the ¾-inch finishing nails.

14. In this step you will carefully bend the ⅛-inch plywood to attach the exterior wall pieces to the top and bottom edges of the outer circles. Apply the waterproof glue to the one exterior wall piece. Position the piece carefully so that the horses and feeder holes are between the dividers; refer to the illustration for details (page 78). Tack the piece into position with the ¾-inch nails. Then glue the other exterior wall piece, fit it into position, and do any trimming necessary for a tight fit. Tack the second piece into place.

15. Cut the four 1-inch dowels to a 3-inch length and slightly round one end of each with sandpaper. Apply the waterproof glue to the collars, and position the collars on the dowels. Allow them to dry thoroughly.

16. Slightly round all the edges of the feeder with sandpaper. Use wood

9. Now check all the parts for fit. After making any necessary corrections, give all the parts a good sanding to remove "fuzz" and slivers and to smooth the surfaces. Don't round any of the edges at this time.

10. Cut colored plastic to fit behind the horse cutouts. Glue them in place with the colored side outward, using the epoxy or silicone glue.

Carousel Bird Feeder

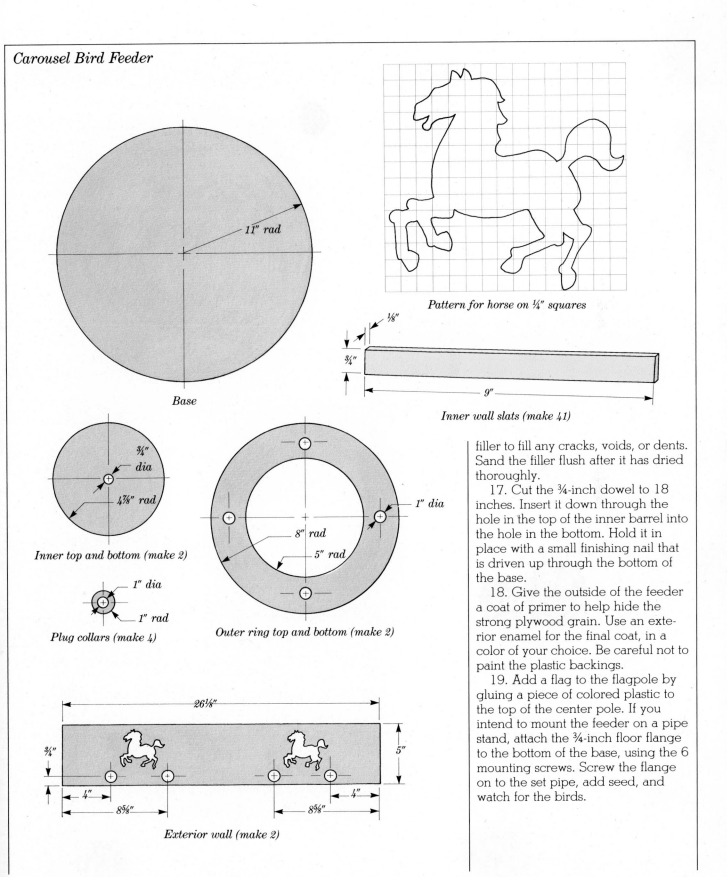

Base

Pattern for horse on ¼" squares

Inner wall slats (make 41)

Inner top and bottom (make 2)

Plug collars (make 4)

Outer ring top and bottom (make 2)

Exterior wall (make 2)

filler to fill any cracks, voids, or dents. Sand the filler flush after it has dried thoroughly.

17. Cut the ¾-inch dowel to 18 inches. Insert it down through the hole in the top of the inner barrel into the hole in the bottom. Hold it in place with a small finishing nail that is driven up through the bottom of the base.

18. Give the outside of the feeder a coat of primer to help hide the strong plywood grain. Use an exterior enamel for the final coat, in a color of your choice. Be careful not to paint the plastic backings.

19. Add a flag to the flagpole by gluing a piece of colored plastic to the top of the center pole. If you intend to mount the feeder on a pipe stand, attach the ¾-inch floor flange to the bottom of the base, using the 6 mounting screws. Screw the flange on to the set pipe, add seed, and watch for the birds.

ALPINE BIRD FEEDER

The Alpine Bird Feeder is designed to hold all common birdseeds. It is an especially effective container for sunflower and pumpkin seeds. The alpine top is actually a cap that comes off so you can refill the feeder.

Description and Tool Requirements

This project can be built with standard hand tools, including a jigsaw. However, a table saw or radial arm saw would greatly facilitate many of the cuts. A hot-melt glue gun is needed. For sanding, a belt sander is desirable. (See "Building Basics," page 18, for tool requirements.)

This feeder can be mounted on a post or a pipe or hung from the corners of the base (see "Building Basics," page 23, for mounting techniques).

Building Steps

1. Look over all the illustrations carefully. If you use a jigsaw to cut the pieces, draw the shapes on the ¼-inch plywood. From the plywood you will cut 4 sets of 2 pieces each.

Saw these pieces by using a radial arm or table saw with a taper jig. Use

The large clear plastic window in the Alpine Bird Feeder lets you quickly see when it needs refilling.

the correct angles shown in the illustrations (pages 82 and 83). These pieces can also be sawn with a hand jigsaw from patterns drawn on the plywood.

Next, cut the window from the ⅛-inch clear plastic. Use a very fine-tooth blade and a slow feed.

2. Saw the window cutout in the plywood front end, as shown in the illustrations (page 83). A jigsaw or band saw can be used for this.

3. To cut the tapering cap, roof top, and roof base from the ¾-inch stock, set the saw angle to 10 degrees. The top should be 2½ by 2⅜ inches and the cap 2⅞ by 3 inches; the base should be 3¾ inches square. See the illustrations for specifics. Note: It might be a good idea to oversize the cap by 1/16 inch and then sand it flush after assembly.

4. Cut the base from a piece of 12-by 12-inch plywood. It is an equal-sided octagon made by cutting the corners off at 45 degrees, 3½ inches in from the corners of the square. Each edge of the octagon should be 5 inches long.

5. Make the rails by ripping 3/16-inch-thick pieces from ¾-inch-thick pine stock. The final dimensions are 3/16 by ¾ inch by 5 inches.

6. If the feeder is to be mounted on a 4 by 4 post, saw the mounting spacer block from a piece of 2 by 4, and the mounting side boards from the ¾-inch stock. If the feeder is to be pipe-mounted or hung, these parts are not needed.

7. With sandpaper, remove the saw marks, especially from the railings and edges of the front and back ends. Sand off any ''fuzz'' or slivers.

8. Check the illustration (page 81) for the placement of the plastic

Alpine Bird Feeder

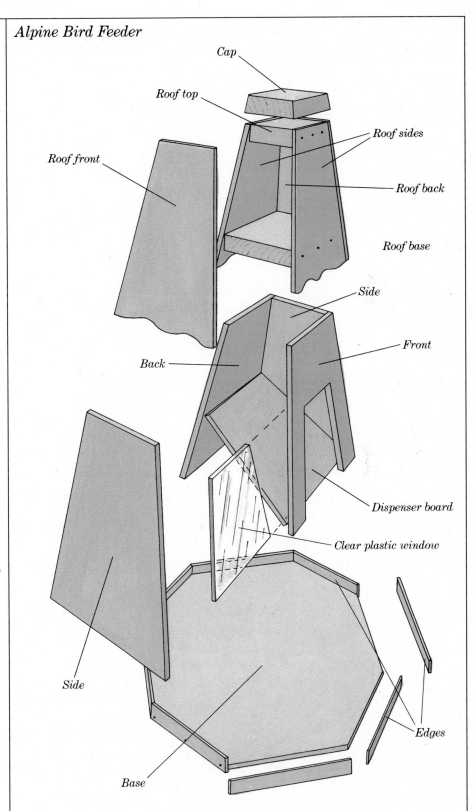

Materials List

ACX (exterior) ¼-inch sanded plywood is the principal construction material. A piece of plywood approximately 2 feet by 3 feet should be more than necessary for all the required pieces. Some small pieces of ¾-inch pine are also required. The 11½-inch square base can come from a scrap of 1 by 12 or the ACX plywood. A small piece of 2 by 4 is needed for the mounting spacer. (See "Building Basics," page 24, for discussion of materials.)

Lumber

Piece	*No. of Pieces*	*Thickness*	*Width*	*Length*
Front and back ends	2	¼″	6½″	8″
Sides	2	¼″	6″	8″
Roof front and back	2	¼″	4″	5½″
Dispenser board	1	¼″	6½″	7″
Roof sides	2	¼″	3⅞″	5½″
Roof cap	1	¾″	2⅞″	3″
Roof top	1	¾″	2½″	2⅜″
Roof base	1	¾″	3¾″	3¾″
Base	1	¼″	12″	12″
Rails	8	3/16″	¾″	5″
Mounting spacer block	1	1½″	3½″	3½″
Mounting side boards	2	¾″	3½″	6″

Hardware and Miscellaneous

Item	*Quantity*	*Size*	*Description*
Clear plastic	1	⅛″ X 6″ X 5″	For the front window
Finishing nails	30 (approx.)	¾″	Galvanized or aluminum
Finishing nails	12 (approx.)	½″	Galvanized or aluminum
Glue	1 small can		Waterproof
Glue	1 or 2 sticks		Hot melt
Sandpaper		80–120 grit	Medium
Finish	1 pint		Exterior primer and paint
Mounting screws	4	2″ X #8	Brass, flat head
Wood filler	¼ pint		
Eye screws	4	⅛″ X 1″	Plated

feeder window. Using hot-melt glue, glue the feeder window in place on the inside of the front end.

9. Assemble the pieces to check the fit. After making any necessary corrections and double-checking placement, begin gluing the assembly, using the waterproof glue. Nail the side, front, and back together using the ¾-inch finishing nails. Note from the illustration (page 81) that the front and back overlap the edges of the sides. Insert the feed dispenser board, and glue it in place, using the hot-melt glue.

10. Using waterproof glue and the ¾-inch finishing nails, glue and nail the roof front and back pieces together, with the roof sides between the front and back. Glue the solid wood cap onto the top of the plywood roof assembly. Glue the roof base inside the assembly, using hot-melt glue.

11. Using a miter saw and box, the miter gauge on the table saw, or the radial arm saw, cut the railing pieces to fit; the miter cut should be 22½ degrees. Glue and tack them into place on the edges of the base by using the ½-inch finishing nails. For a tight fit, cut and fasten as you go. Drive the brads in flush with the railing surface.

Alpine Bird Feeder

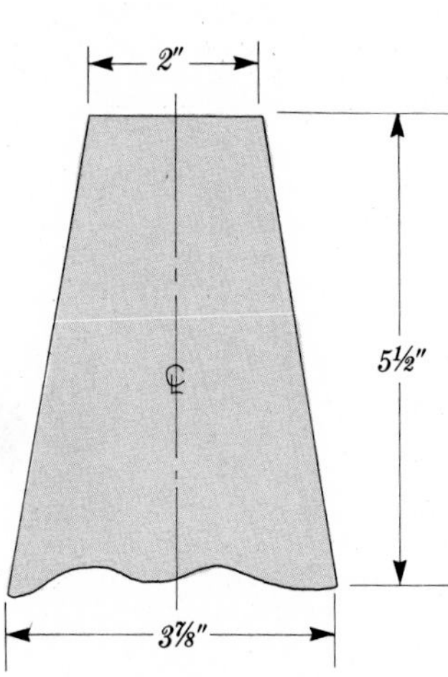

Roof sides (make 2)

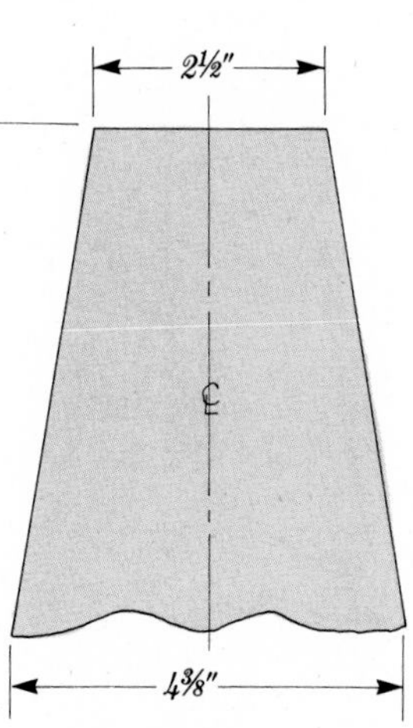

Roof front and back (make 2)

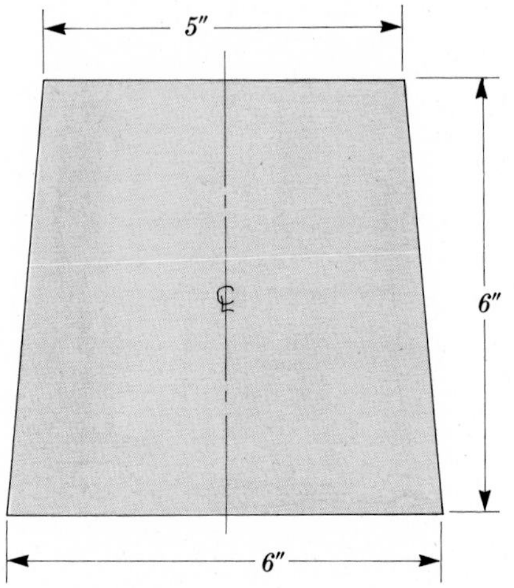

Dispenser board

12. Now give the entire assembly a good sanding. A belt sander would be very useful for this. Sand the roof assembly and the edges of the feeder so the pieces are flush. Sand the edges of the base. Using a vibrating pad sander or a sanding block, smooth the inside surface of the base.

13. If the feeder is to be post-mounted, use the waterproof glue and screws to fasten the mounting spacer block to the bottom of the base. Glue the feeder to the base, using the hot-melt glue. Place the glue neatly into the space between the slight angle on the bottom edge of the feeder and the base.

14. To help mask the strong plywood grain, use a primer paint on the outside before the exterior paint is applied. Use subdued colors; many birds don't like the bright ones.

Alpine Bird Feeder

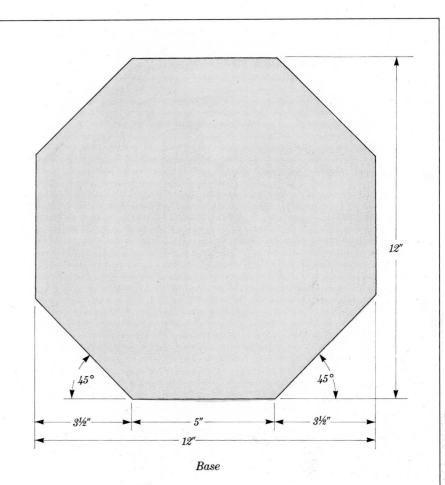

Base

Front and back
(make 2—cut window in front only)

Sides (make 2)

Clear plastic window

WINDOW COAXING FEEDER

This project allows you to bird-watch in the comfort of your home. You can watch a variety of birds come to your window to sample the seeds that you put out for them to enjoy. This project has two feeder units. You can put sunflower seeds at one end and another variety of seeds at the other.

Description and Tool Requirements

The Window Coaxing Feeder requires the use of a table or radial arm saw, along with a power jigsaw or band saw, a drill, and standard hand tools. In addition, you need a 3/16-inch drill bit, some clamps, and a countersink; pilot bits for the screws cited in the materials list would be useful.

The feeder is designed to be mounted against the side of the house under a window. Before you start the project, select the window. Make sure it can be opened easily—especially in winter when storm windows could get in the way. Make sure you will be able to open the window without hitting the feeder and that the feeder can be attached to the side of the house easily. You may have to adjust the design or the mounting hardware to fasten the feeder to brick, bevel siding, or the like. The overall length of the feeder can be adjusted to fit the location, so check the mounting site in advance and determine the size needed.

Because this feeder will be easily seen from the inside of the house, it should be built carefully. Make sure all the pieces fit tightly and are square, and work carefully to ensure that the finish is attractive—something you will be proud to show off to your friends.

From the comfort of your home during cold months, you can enjoy watching feeding birds close up with the Window Coaxing Feeder.

Building Steps

1. Choose a smooth-cut carbide or steel cabinet blade for your radial arm saw or table saw. From the 1 by 8, cut a 25-inch blank for the base. Make this piece longer or shorter to fit the window location. If you plan to make the railings yourself, cut them now by ripping two ½-inch-wide strips off the side of the blank. Don't use a blade with a kerf over ⅛ inch—the base piece will be too narrow. If you plan to use precut moldings instead of home-cut railings, continue to step 2.

2. Rip the 25-inch base blank to the final width, 6 inches.

3. From what remains of the 1 by 8, cut the lids, backs, and mounting blocks, 2 of each. Also cut the blanks for the 4 side pieces and 2 support blocks. Then cut the 2 dispenser boards from the ¼-inch plywood or hardboard.

4. In this step you will use a radial arm saw or a taper jig on a table saw to cut the 1-inch taper, or slope, on the 4 side pieces. Study the illustrations to learn how the angles should look. Then, draw the cut line on the first piece. Carefully cut *outside* the line to make sure the angle is correct. Make any adjustments necessary. When you are satisfied with the result of test-cutting, cut the final slope on all 4 side pieces.

5. Study the illustration (page 86) to see how the slots in the slanted sides should hold the glass or plastic fronts. Each slot should be ⅛ inch wide and ⁵⁄₁₆ inch deep. Note that you have 2 pieces for the left and 2 pieces for the right. Before cutting, match up the pieces in each pair. If any piece has a surface defect, turn it so the defect will be on the inside of the feeder. To prevent cutting the slot in the wrong side, mark the pieces to help you distinguish right from left and inside from outside.

Each groove should be ¼ inch from the edge, so use a temporary stop on a radial arm saw and set the saw depth for ⁵⁄₁₆ inch. If using a table saw, set the fence ¼ inch from the inside of the blade.

Window Coaxing Feeder

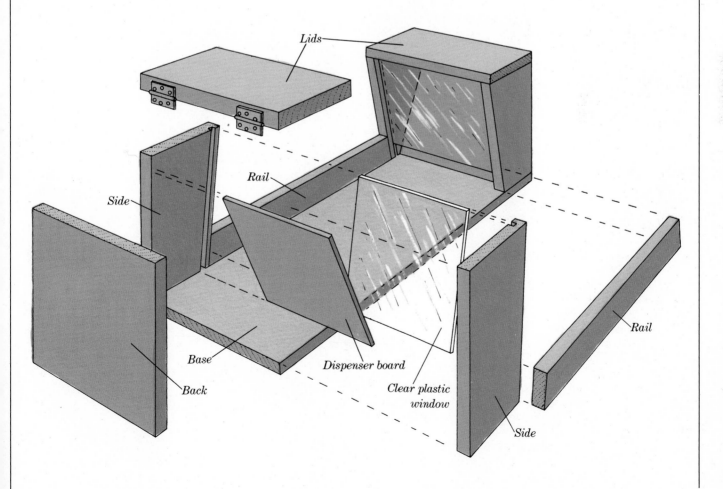

Window Coaxing Feeder

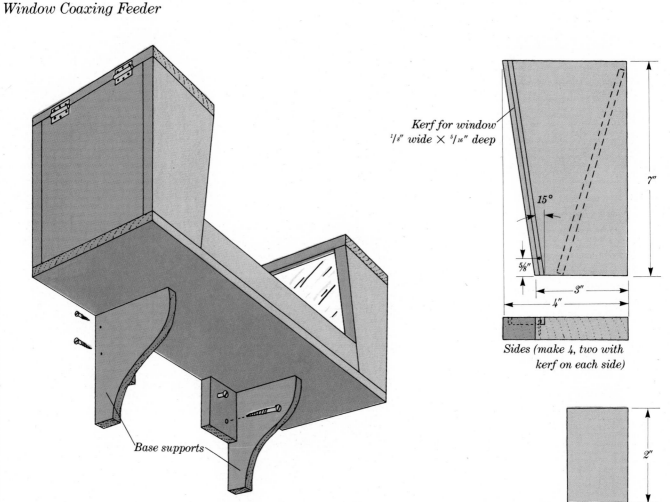

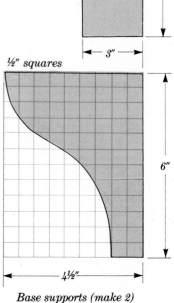

Kerf for window
⅛″ wide × ⁵/₁₆″ deep

15°

7″

⅝″

3″

4″

*Sides (make 4, two with
kerf on each side)*

2″

3″

½″ squares

6″

4½″

Base supports (make 2)

Make the cuts parallel to the sloping edge. Try slipping the glass or plastic into the slots. If the slots are too tight, reset the stop or fence and resaw the slots.

6. There is one more sawing operation; it requires a jigsaw or a band saw, using a narrow smooth-cut blade. Using a grid, transfer the pattern for the supports from the illustration onto one of the support blanks. Temporarily join the 2 blanks together as described in "Building Basics," page 21, in the section about duplicate cutting. Gang-saw the curved shape. While the 2 pieces are still joined together, sand the edges

smooth. A drum or belt sander works well for this. After sanding, separate the 2 supports.

7. Give all the pieces a thorough sanding by hand to round the edges. Start with medium-grit sandpaper, then move to fine-grit paper.

8. Drive a ¾-inch finishing nail into the center of each kerf groove, ⅝ inch from the base of the groove. Hammer the brads down so they are flush with the outside surface. They will act as stops for the window fronts, allowing a ⅝-inch opening at the bottom for seed flow.

9. Test the pieces for fit. If all dimensions are correct and the pieces square, you are ready for assembly.

A word of caution before you start: Many waterproof glues are dark in color and will stain wood. These stains are especially unsightly if a clear finish is used. So, when you apply the glue, be prudent. Immediately wash off any oozes or smears with a sponge and warm water, and lightly sand the area after the glue has dried.

10. Partially assemble the feeder boxes, gluing and nailing the sides flush with the backs. Use several temporary spreader blocks or sticks cut exactly 4½ inches long to keep the box sides in square. Use clamps if necessary. Before the glue sets, slide the windows up and down in the slots, making sure the windows are free to move. Measure to make sure that the grooved edges of the sides are 4½ inches apart.

11. Turn the boxes upside down on the workbench. Set the base on them and position it correctly (leave the temporary spreaders in if necessary). Use glue and nails to fasten the base to the boxes. Take care to place the nails properly, so they don't split the sides or ends of the boxes. Clean off excess glue quickly as described in step 9.

12. After the glue has dried, set the assembly right side up. You now need to nail in the dispenser boards, using the ¾-inch finishing nails. Slope them as shown in the illustration (page 85).

13. Glue and nail the support pieces to the bottom of the base. Holding the supports one at a time in a well-padded vise will facilitate assembly. Place the nails carefully, so they don't split the sides or ends. Let the glue dry.

14. Position the mounting blocks on edge, between the base and supports (see the illustration on page 86). Clamp the blocks in place. Through the base and in from the side through the supports, drill pilot holes for the 1¼-inch screws. Countersink the pilot holes. Apply glue, and drive the screws so the heads are flush with the surface.

(see the illustration on page 86)

Materials List

Surfaced western red cedar or redwood is the preferred wood, though soft pine can be used instead. Plan to varnish cedar or redwood; use primer and paint to finish pine. Purchase approximately 6 feet of 1 by 8 stock. The 1 by 8 should be of good grade and relatively free of large knots or other defects. Plan to cut the pieces from between slight defects. If you plan to cut the railings yourself, make sure the 1 by 8 is at least 7¼ inches wide. Precut molding can be substituted for square-edged railings that you cut yourself. Choose a ¾-inch quarter-round or half-round, a ¾-inch cove design, or any similar molding that appeals to you. Two pieces of ¼-inch plywood or hardboard are needed for the dispenser boards. (See "Building Basics," page 24, for discussion of materials.)

Lumber

Piece	No. of Pieces	Thickness	Width	Length
Base	1	¾"	6"	25" (approx.)
Railing*	2	¾"	½"	18⅞"
Lids	2	¾"	4"	6"
Backs	2	¾"	4½"	7"
Mounting blocks	2	¾"	2"	3"
Sides	4	¾"	4"	7"
Support blocks	2	¾"	4½"	6"
Dispenser boards	2	¼"	4⅝"	7½"

* Railings must be cut from a 1 by 8 that is at least 7¼ inches wide.

Hardware and Miscellaneous

Item	Quantity	Size	Description
Finishing nails	25	1½"	Galvanized or aluminum
Finishing nails	16	¾"	Galvanized or aluminum
Glue	1 small can		Waterproof
Sandpaper	2 sheets	100–150 grit	Medium and fine
Finish	1 pint		Polyurethane varnish or primer and paint
Wood filler	¼ pint		Matching wood color
Windows	2	⅛" × 5" × 6½"	Plastic or glass
Screws	6	2" × #8 or #9	Brass, flat head
Screws	6	1¼" × #6	Brass, flat head
Hinges	4	¾" × 1"	Brass, with screws
Feeder fronts	2	5⅛" × 6½"	⅛" glass or clear plastic
Screw eyes	2	⅛" × ½"	Brass or plated

15. Next, using a miter cut, saw the railings to fit snugly between the 2 feeder boxes (see the illustration on page 85 for details). Glue and nail the railings into place.

16. The lids will be attached to the backs by means of brass hinges. With the hinge screws, attach the hinges to the ends of the lid pieces. Carefully position the lids, and fasten the other flap of the hinges to the backs of the feeder boxes.

17. Slide the plastic or glass fronts down into the slots. They should slide easily down to the brad stops.

18. Give the feeder one more sanding. If you used cedar or redwood, finish the outside of the feeder with at least 2 coats of varnish. If you used pine, paint the feeder.

19. To mount the feeder, drill pilot holes for 2-inch screws through the lower part of the supports and the mounting blocks. (This can be done before finishing if you desire.) Refer to the illustration (page 86) for correct positions. Countersink the holes and use the 2-inch screws to fasten the feeder to the side of the house.

(see the illustration on page 85 for details)

WEATHER VANE FEEDER

This feeder is designed to always face the wind—one look in your backyard will tell you what direction the breeze is blowing. An added benefit is that feeding birds will be protected because the feeder acts as a windbreak.

Description and Tool Requirements

If you have the standard hand tools, a power jigsaw, and a drill, you can make the Weather Vane Feeder. However, one or more stationary power tools—including a table saw, band saw, or scroll saw—would give better results. The project requires a countersink and ⅛-, ¼-, ¹³/₁₆-, and 1-inch drill bits. A wood rasp and a coping saw would be useful.

This feeder must be post-mounted (see "Building Basics," page 23, for mounting techniques).

Building Steps

1. Start by cutting 2 pieces, 27 inches long, from the 1 by 12; these pieces are the side boards. On one of the pieces, lightly draw a grid of 1-inch squares. Then expand and transfer the side board outline from the illustration. Temporarily join the 2 pieces for gang-sawing (see "Building Basics," page 21, for discussion of duplicate cutting). Carefully saw the shape, using a hand jigsaw or a band saw. Sand the edges smooth. Use a belt sander if available.

The Weather Vane Feeder will swing to face the wind and provide a windbreak for feeding birds.

Weather Vane Feeder

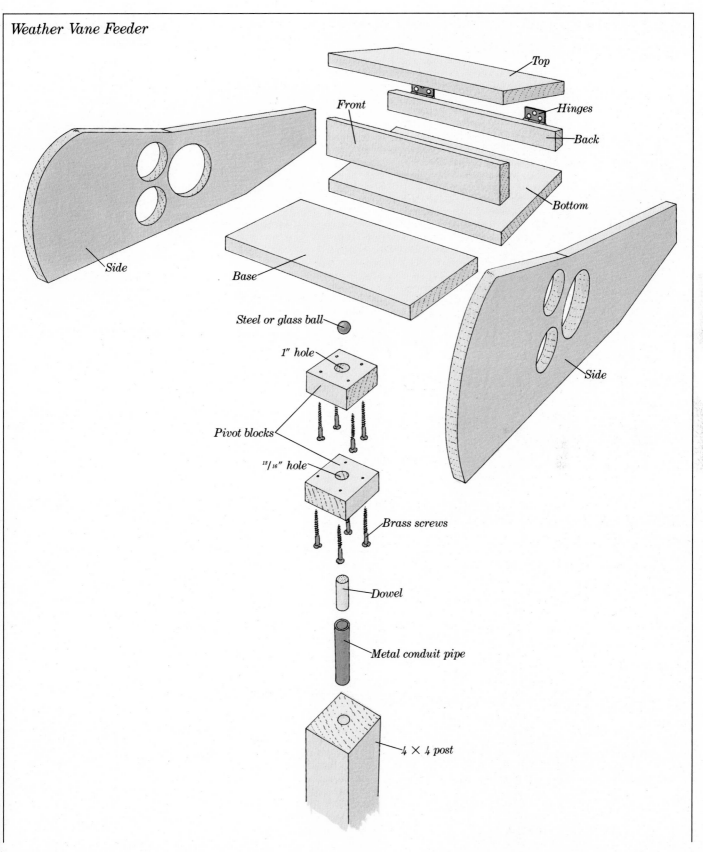

Top

Hinges

Front

Back

Bottom

Side

Base

Steel or glass ball

1" hole

Pivot blocks

$^{13}/_{16}$" hole

Brass screws

Dowel

Metal conduit pipe

4 × 4 post

Materials List

Western red cedar, redwood, or soft pine are excellent materials for this project. All lumber should be relatively free of large knots and other defects. Purchase one 1 by 12, approximately 8 feet long. Several small pieces of softwood 2 by 4 are also required. For the mounting post you will need a treated 4 by 4. (See "Building Basics," page 24, for discussion of materials.)

Lumber

Piece	No. of Pieces	Thickness	Width	Length
Side boards	2	¾"	11¼"	27"
Top and bottom	2	¾"	9¾"	11¼"
Front	1	¾"	3⅜"	11¼"
Back	2	¾"	1"	11¼"
Base	1	¾"	6"	11¼"
Pivot blocks	2	1½"	3½"	3½"
Post (treated)	1	3½"	3½"	60" (approx.)

Hardware and Miscellaneous

Item	Quantity	Size	Description
Finishing nails	25	1½"	Galvanized or aluminum
Glue	¼ cup		Waterproof
Sandpaper	1 sheet	80–120 grit	Medium
Finish	1 pint		Exterior oil stain or paint
Screws	4	2½" × #6	Brass or coated drywall
Screws	4	3" × #8 or #9	Brass or coated drywall
Hinges	2	1" × 2"	Brass, with screws
Hook and eye	1	³/₁₆"	Brass or plated
Dowel	1	⅝" × 3"	
Steel ball*	1	1" dia.	
Pipe	1	¾" × 12"	Metal conduit
Grease or petroleum jelly	3 tbsp.		
Wood preservative	Small amount		

* A 1-inch glass marble can be substituted.

---

2. Refer to the illustration on page 91 to learn the placement and diameters of the three decorative holes in the side pieces. With the pieces still joined, lay out the 3 holes by using a compass (or a pencil tied to a string anchored by a tack). If you have a drill bit large enough to drill the holes, use it. Most do-it-yourselfers will have to saw the hole, however. To do so, predrill a ¼-inch saw-access hole inside each circle. Saw the hole, using a coping saw, scroll saw, or jigsaw. If you use a jigsaw, use a very narrow smooth-cut blade. Smooth the holes with the round side of a wood rasp or sandpaper. Now the 2 side boards can be separated.

3. Using a table saw or a radial arm saw (if available), cut the top and bottom boards. Note the 13-degree beveled edges on both pieces.

4. Now cut the front and back pieces. Both pieces are ripped with a 13-degree bevel on both sides. Finally, cut the base with square edges (see the illustration on page 91).

5. From 2 by 4 stock, measure and cut the 2 pivot blocks.

6. That completes the sawing. Prior to assembly, give all the pieces a thorough sanding to smooth the surfaces and round the edges.

7. Assemble the complete unit to check the fit. Make any corrections necessary. When all dimensions are correct and the pieces are in square,

use glue and the finishing nails to fasten the pieces together. Remember, do not nail down the top piece. In addition, be sure to align the front piece to the top edge of the sides; retain the opening at the bottom so the seed can flow. Keep the illustrations on pages 89 and 91 close at hand while putting the feeder together and refer to them often to make sure all the pieces are in the correct position. They will be hard to move once the glue is dry.

8. Attach the hinges to the top board and the back piece. Use the hinges to fasten the top to the back. Screw in the hook and eye to hold the top in place.

9. Drill a 1-inch hole through the center of one of the pivot blocks. Drill a ¹³/₁₆-inch hole through the center of the other one. In each block predrill 4 holes for the 2½-inch screws (see the illustration on page 89); do not drill the screw holes in identical locations on both blocks. Use a piece of scrap lumber under the blocks to prevent splitting when the drill emerges. Countersink the screws.

10. Now you must find the center of balance for the feeder. Put the pivot block with the 1-inch hole near the edge of a table and set the unit on it. Shift the feeder until you find the best balance point. Mark the block location on the base of the feeder.

11. Turn the feeder over. At the marked location, glue the block with the 1-inch hole to the base. In addition, fasten the block with the four 2½-inch screws. The screw heads should be slightly below the surface.

12. When the glue is dry, carefully fill the hole with petroleum jelly, being careful not to get any on the surfaces. Now, drop the 1-inch steel ball or marble in the hole. Glue and screw the block with the ¹³/₁₆-inch hole on top of the first block. Use the four 3-inch screws for this assembly. If you are in an area with high winds,

Weather Vane Feeder

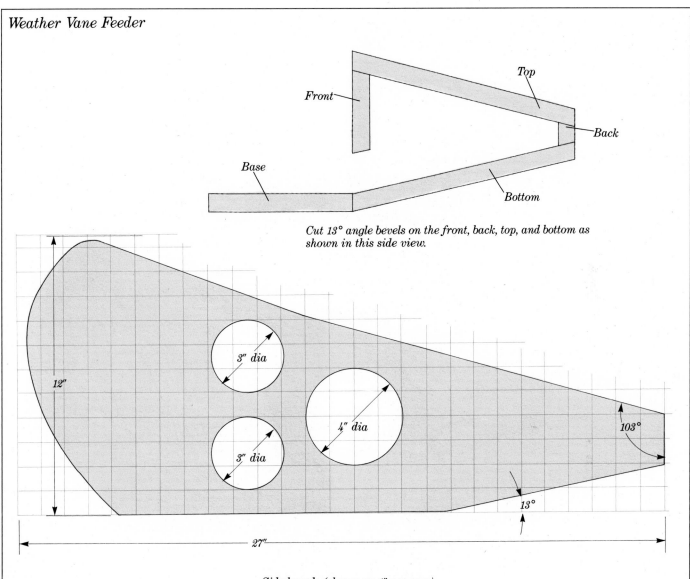

Cut 13° angle bevels on the front, back, top, and bottom as shown in this side view.

Side boards (shown on 1" squares)

add another block with a $^{13}/_{16}$-inch hole to prevent the feeder from being blown off the swivel.

13. Give the feeder a final sanding. Finish the outside with exterior oil stain or paint.

14. Now for mounting: In the center of the top of the treated 4 by 4

mounting post, drill a ¾-inch hole approximately 6 inches deep. Set the post in the ground at the desired location, making sure it is plumb. Treat the end grain and the hole with brush-on wood preservative.

15. Place the ⅝-inch dowel into the metal conduit pipe so that 1 inch sticks out the end. If the fit is tight, you may have to drive the dowel

through the tube. If the fit is too loose, drill a small hole through the pipe and hammer in a small nail to hold the dowel in place. Grease the whole assembly well, and place it in the hole in the post. Set the feeder down on the protruding pin and give it a push to be sure it swings freely.

COUNTRY GAZEBO FEEDER

*T**his gazebo feeder will make a handsome addition to your garden. Many varieties of birds will want to visit this special feeder. The unique design has a clear feed container that tells you at a glance when it's time to refill it. It contains enough seed for it to go for quite some time before restocking is needed.*

Description and Tool Requirements

This attractive feeder is somewhat intricate; it requires some skill with woodworking tools. In addition to the standard hand-held tools, a table saw and a band saw are required. Other tools that are or may be needed include a drill with ⅛-, ¼-, and ³⁄₁₆-inch bits; a jigsaw, coping saw, or scroll saw; a hot-melt glue gun; a staple gun; and several bar and C-clamps. A #8–32 threading die and a propane torch are also required.

There are a number of thin and narrow pieces in this feeder. Sawing them will bring fingers close to moving saw blades. Take care; use push sticks and hold-downs. (See "Building Basics," page 20, on tool requirements and safe sawing techniques.)

This handsome feeder will complement any backyard and should attract many feathered visitors.

This feeder is designed to be hung from a wire attached to the eyed rod in the middle. It can also be mounted on a deck railing, a post, or a pipe stand. (See "Building Basics," page 23, for mounting methods and parts requirements.)

Building Steps

1. If your lumber is narrower than 1 by 12, you must edge-glue 2 pieces to form the base. Using your table or radial arm saw, cut 2 pieces of ¾-inch stock to 6 inches by 12 inches. Joint the edges and edge-glue them, using the waterproof glue and your bar or pipe clamps. Trim the base piece to 11¼ inches square after the glue has completely dried.

If you are using a 1 by 12, cut it to form an 11¼-inch square.

2. The 1½-inch-thick chimney can be made from 2 pieces of 2 by 4, or 4 pieces of ¾-inch material. Cut to create two 3½- by 5½-inch blanks. Face-glue and clamp the blanks. When dry, cut them to final size: 2⅞ by 3 by 5 inches. After drilling a ³⁄₁₆-inch hole down through the center, put this piece aside for future machining.

3. While you are at the saw, cut the ¼-inch plywood into 2 pieces for the roof. Refer to the illustration (page 96), then cut the chimney openings 3 inches wide and 2¼ inches deep in the center of one edge of each roof piece. Use a jigsaw or band saw for this operation.

4. Check the illustration (page 95) for the correct roof-slope angle. Then, using the table saw, cut 2 gable ends from ¾-inch solid stock, each 11¼ inches wide with a center peak 5 inches high.

5. Rip the four ¾-inch square corner posts from the lumber. Check the illustration (page 96) at this time. Notice that the 4 posts are relieved on 2 sides at the top so that the soffits can fit flush. Mount a dado blade on your saw and make these crosscuts, ¼ inch deep and ⅞ inch wide.

6. In this step you will cut the roof trim, chimney trim (side and bottom), the soffit blanks, and the railing blanks. These should be cut on a table saw; however, a band saw with a fine-cut blade can also be used. Use caution when sawing any thin or narrow pieces.

The thickness of the stock can be reduced easily by using a cabinet planer if one is available. Lacking a planer, the next best and next safest way to cut these pieces is to first resaw the ¾-inch stock down to the necessary thickness. Then rip the desired pieces to size and crosscut them to exact length. A band saw is an excellent tool to use for resawing. A table saw can also be used if used with care. In either case, use a smooth-cut saw blade.

Now, using one of the preceding techniques, saw the various pieces. Cut the railing blanks slightly overlength. They can be cut to fit during assembly.

7. In this step you will saw out the chimney stops and the feed container frames. Notice several things before making these cuts. First, the chimney stops have one edge beveled. Set the saw to 40 degrees for the bevel rip cuts. Second, the feed container frames have a compound miter of 10 degrees at one end of each piece. To achieve this, square-cut the frame pieces to approximately 11 inches. Then make the compound crosscut with both the miter gauge and saw blade set 10 degrees off perpendicular; the long side of these pieces should be 9¾ inches. Check the illustrations carefully for the details and dimensions.

8. Cut the clear plastic feed dispenser windows while you are still at the table or band saw. The ⅛-inch plastic can be sawn using a fine-tooth blade. Hold the plastic firmly on the table to prevent chatter, and feed slowly. The 4 plastic pieces, 8¾ inches long, are trapezoids, tapering evenly from 4 inches at the base to 2 inches at the top.

9. Now, cut the window grooves (kerfs) in the 4 feed container frames. Use a saw blade in your table saw that has a kerf of ⅛ inch or slightly larger. Set the blade depth at ³⁄₁₆ inch. Saw 2 slots on opposite edges of each frame piece, down the center. Be sure to orient the grooved sides to the long end of the mitered cut end so the windows are positioned correctly when the feed dispenser is assembled. Check the sides carefully against the illustration (page 96) before making the cuts.

Fit the ⅛-inch plastic windows in the kerf groove. If the slot is too tight, make a second pass across the saw, with the fence very slightly offset. This should widen the groove so the plastic will fit.

10. Get out your coping saw or scroll saw. Stack and temporarily join the railing blanks for gang-sawing (see the section on duplicate cutting in "Building Basics," page 21). Draw the railing pattern on the top railing blank. Drill a ¼-inch saw-access hole inside the cutout portion of the rail design. Carefully saw the interior. A jigsaw or band saw with a very narrow blade can also be used for making this and the curved cuts in step 11. If a band saw is used, the kerf cut used to enter the inside cutout of the railings will have to be glued back together.

11. Stack, temporarily join, and trace the pattern using carbon paper on the soffit blanks. Then gang-saw the curved soffit designs. Separate the railing and soffit pieces.

12. Set all the pieces together on your workbench and check for fit. Use the illustration (page 94) to check placement. If the dimensions and assembly are correct, give all the pieces a sanding to remove the saw

marks, "fuzz," and splinters and to smooth the surfaces. Fill any edge voids in the plywood with wood filler. Let the filler dry completely before sanding it flush.

13. Drill 4 screw pilot holes in the corners of the base; see the illustrations for exact placement. Countersink these screw holes. Drill a 3/16-inch hole in the center of the base piece.

14. Predrill pilot holes up into the base of the post to prevent splitting. Begin the assembly by gluing with the waterproof glue and using screws to fasten the 4 corner posts in place, flush with each corner. Be sure to position the posts so that the top dadoes for the soffits are on the outside edges. Again, refer to the illustration on this page.

Note: If the Country Gazebo Feeder is to be finished with an oil stain, glue smear will show through. Use the waterproof glue judiciously throughout assembly, and clean up any ooze or smear quickly with a sponge and warm water.

Lightly sand when dry.

15. Now fit the 4 railings into position. They were cut slightly overlength and may need some trimming to achieve a snug fit between the posts. Glue the railings with the waterproof glue and tack them into place using 1-inch finishing nails.

16. Glue and nail the soffits in place on top of the posts with the 1-inch finishing nails. Install the longer ones first, then size the others to fit.

17. In this step you will glue and nail the gables in place on top of the posts with the ¾-inch finishing nails. To help prevent splitting, partially predrill the nail holes before assembling the pieces. Hot-melt glue may be in order to hold the gables in place initially. Nail down through the corners of the gables into the top of the posts, being careful not to split anything.

18. Use hot-melt glue to assemble the feed container. Insert the clear plastic sides into the slots in the sides

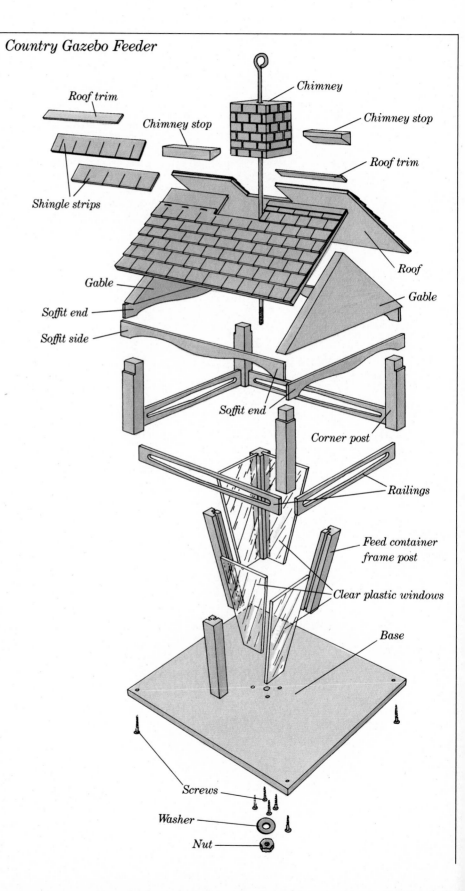

Country Gazebo Feeder

Roof trim

Chimney

Chimney stop

Chimney stop

Roof trim

Shingle strips

Roof

Gable

Gable

Soffit end

Soffit side

Soffit end

Corner post

Railings

Feed container frame post

Clear plastic windows

Base

Screws

Washer

Nut

of the container frames. In the lower, or narrow, end, leave a ½-inch space (leave a ¾-inch gap if sunflower seeds are to be used).

Position the container in the center of the base, and mark the frame positions. For the screws, drill pilot holes down through the base at a 10-degree angle to match the slope of the container frames. Countersink the holes on the bottom of the base. Apply the hot-melt glue to the base and fasten the feed container into position with screws.

19. Now use the waterproof glue to hold the 2 roof boards into place on top of the gables. They should overhang the gable ends 1¼ inches. Be sure the chimney openings are aligned. Now nail the roof boards into position with the 1-inch nails. Note: The feed container is not attached to the roof or top. It is held only at the bottom by the screws inserted in the previous step.

20. Pause in the assembly operations to make the shingles. Using the table or radial arm saw, crosscut the 1 by 12 to make eight 2-inch strips. The grain should be running crosswise. If there is any appreciable cup or warp in the strips, cut them in two, with one piece 7 inches long.

Now move to the band saw and tilt the table 1 or 2 degrees. The shingle strips are going to be sliced from the

2-inch pieces by sawing them on edge. Set the band saw fence (or clamp a guide) so that the thick edge of the shingle strip will be 3/32 inch thick. Use a resaw blade, ½ inch or wider. Be sure to use a push stick to move the pieces past the blade. Reverse the material on each pass. Each piece of ¾-inch stock should yield 6 shingle strips. You will need at least 38 strips, 7 inches or longer.

Returning to the table saw, stack about ⅓ of the sawn shingle strips thick side down, offsetting half of them ½ inch. Carefully holding them

together, cut a series of ⅛-inch kerfs, 1 inch deep and 1 inch apart, to simulate individual shingles. Then do the same thing with the rest of the shingle strips.

21. Place a layer of shingle strips along one of the eaves of the roof, allowing a ¼-inch overhang. Double up the first layer. Tack down the strip, using staples, the hot-melt glue, or both. Place the next row on top of the first strips as shown in the illustrations. Separate the 2 rows by 1 inch, aligning one row on top of the kerfs. Stagger the kerf slots so that one is over the center of the slot below it.

Country Gazebo Feeder

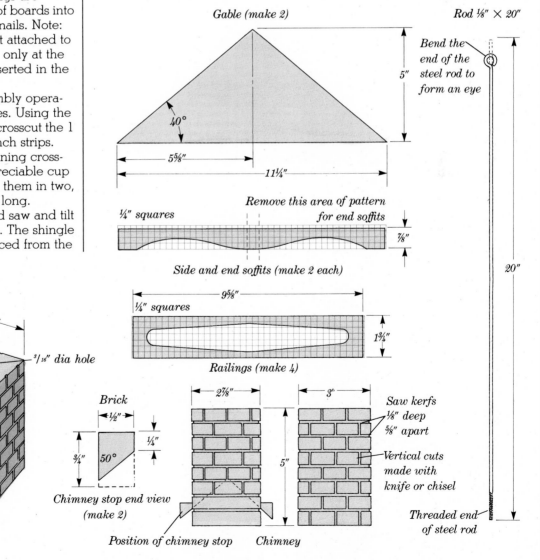

Gable (make 2)

Rod ⅛" × 20"

Bend the end of the steel rod to form an eye

5"

40°

5⅝"

11¼"

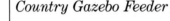

Remove this area of pattern for end soffits

¼" squares

⅞"

Side and end soffits (make 2 each)

9⅝"

¼" squares

1¾"

Railings (make 4)

20"

3"

2⅞"

3/16" dia hole

5"

Brick

½"

¾"

50°

¼"

Chimney stop end view (make 2)

2⅞"

3"

5"

Saw kerfs ⅛" deep ⅝" apart

Vertical cuts made with knife or chisel

Threaded end of steel rod

Position of chimney stop   Chimney

Country Gazebo Feeder

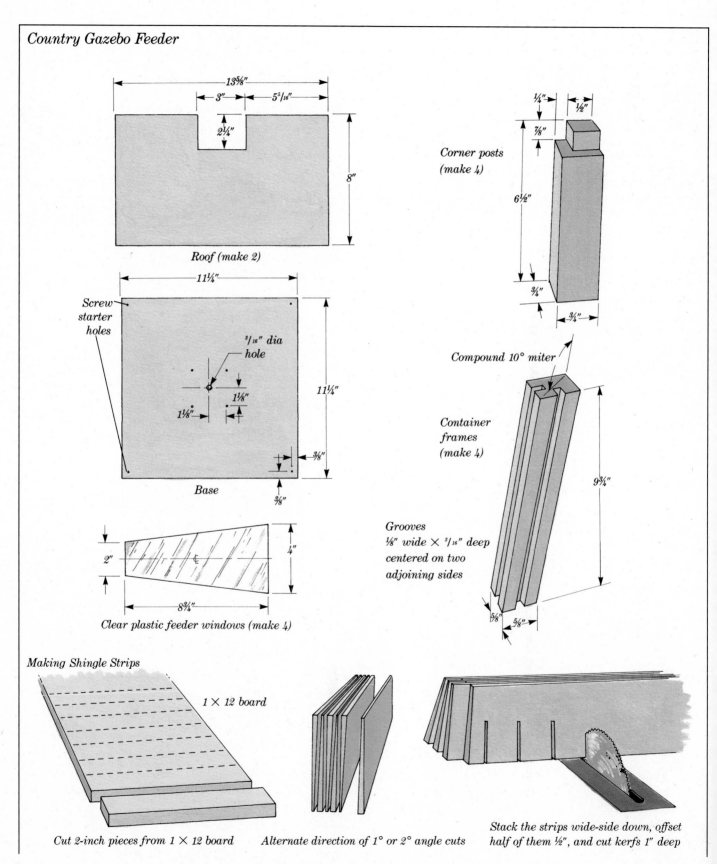

13⅝"
3" **5⁵/₁₆"**
2¼"
8"

Roof (make 2)

11¼"

Screw starter holes

³/₁₆" dia hole

11¼"

1⅛"
1⅛"
⅜"
⅜"

Base

2"
4"
8¾"

Clear plastic feeder windows (make 4)

Corner posts (make 4)

¼"
½"
⅞"
6½"
¾"
¾"

Compound 10° miter

Container frames (make 4)

9¾"

Grooves ⅛" wide × ³/₁₆" deep centered on two adjoining sides

⅝" **⅝"**

Making Shingle Strips

1 × 12 board

Cut 2-inch pieces from 1 × 12 board

Alternate direction of 1° or 2° angle cuts

Stack the strips wide-side down, offset half of them ½", and cut kerfs 1" deep

Fasten the strip into place. Continue to do this, working up to the ridge. Cut the strips to length as you go, or use a sharp knife to trim along the gable ends and the chimney. Finish shingling the rest of the roof.

22. Now, get the chimney block. Check to make sure it fits easily through the opening in the top of the roof pieces. Using your table saw, cut four ⅛-inch-wide kerfs around the chimney. The kerfs should be ⅛ inch deep and spaced at ⅝ inch. Check the illustration (page 95) for placement. These slots are to simulate horizontal lines of a brick wall. Using a small chisel or wood-carving tool, cut vertical slots at 1-inch intervals to complete the "brick" outline. Stagger these vertical cuts as in the illustration (page 95).

23. Check the chimney details in the illustration (page 95). With the waterproof glue, glue the chimney stops in place on the chimney; then nail them using the ¾-inch nails.

24. Find the ⅛-inch-diameter steel rod. If the rod still needs threading, get out your tap and die set. Holding the rod in a jawed vise, thread one of the ends by using an #8-32 NC die. Leave the rod in the vise. With a stout pair of needle-nose pliers handy, heat the unthreaded end with a propane torch until it becomes cherry red. Bend the end to form an eye.

25. After the rod has thoroughly cooled, slide the threaded end down through the chimney. Screw on one #8-32 nut. Add a washer, then slide the end through the hole in the center of the base. Add another washer and nut and tighten. Check the illustration (page 94) for details.

The chimney is, of course, the cover for the feed container. Slide it up the rod, and the hole in the roof provides the means to fill the feeder with seed.

26. Add roof and chimney trim. Check the fit and make any necessary corrections. Then glue the trim into place.

Materials List

Western red cedar or redwood are the preferred woods for this project. The base is designed to come from a piece of surfaced 1 by 12. However, if that piece is made from edge-glued stock, narrower lumber can be used. Approximately 5 lineal feet of 1 by 12 or the equivalent in narrower 1-by stock is needed; the exact amount depends on the frequency of knots. All parts should come from wood free of knots or defects. This project also calls for a piece of ¼-inch ACX (exterior) plywood, 9 by 28 inches. The chimney can be made from a ¾- or 1½-inch 2 by 4. (See "Building Basics," page 24, for discussion of materials.)

Lumber

Piece	*No. of Pieces*	*Thickness*	*Width*	*Length*
Base	1	¾"	11¼"	11¼"
Chimney	1	2⅞"	3"	5"
Roof	2	¼" plywood	8"	13⅜"
Gable ends	2	¾"	5"	11¼"
Corner posts	4	¾"	¾"	6½"
Trim, roof	4	⅛"	⅝"	5¾"
Trim, chimney (side)	4	⅛"	⅝"	2¼"
Trim, chimney (bottom)	2	⅛"	⅝"	2⅞"
Soffit (ends)	2	¼"	⅞"	10⅝"
Soffit (sides)	2	¼"	⅞"	11⅛"
Railings	4	½"	1¾"	9⅝"
Stops, chimney	2	½"	¾"	2⅞"
Feed container frames	4	⅝"	⅝"	9¾"
Shingle strips	38	3/32"	2"	7"

Hardware and Miscellaneous

Item	*Quantity*	*Size*	*Description*
⅛" clear plastic	4	4" X 8¾"	For the dispenser windows
Finishing nails	20	1"	Galvanized or aluminum
Finishing nails	40	¾"	Galvanized or aluminum
Staples	50	⅜"	Aluminum or coated
Glue	1 small can		Waterproof
Glue	2 sticks		Hot melt
Wood filler	1 tube		
Sandpaper		80–120 grit	Medium
Finish	1 pint		Exterior oil stain or satin varnish
Nut	1	#8–32	
Washers	2	#8–32	
Screws	8	1¼" X #6	Brass, flat head or coated drywall
Rod, steel	1	⅛" X 20"	Threaded one end, with nuts and washers
Wire	1	Stranded	Galvanized, for hanging

27. Give the entire assembly a light sanding to remove remaining "fuzz," splinters, or glue.

28. Finish the shingled roof of the gazebo feeder with several coats of an oil stain or an exterior satin varnish to bring out the wood grain and color and to provide the necessary weather protection. For a pleasing contrast paint the rest of the feeder with a light-colored exterior paint; otherwise, stain the entire feeder.

29. Hang the feeder by using sturdy galvanized wire. If a base mount is preferred, refer to the discussion on mounting in "Building Basics," page 23.

COUNTRY STORE FEEDER

T his attractive feeder is based upon the old storefront design, with two windows on both sides of the entranceway. The birdseed feeds down onto the floor through small openings under the windows. This is an easy weekend project.

Description and Tool Requirements

This project can be built with standard hand tools. However, because most of the cuts are straight and square, a table saw or radial arm saw would be best for cutting most of the pieces and ensuring a snug final fit. A jigsaw, coping saw, or scroll saw is needed for the inside window cuts in the front. A hot-melt glue gun would come in handy. (See "Building Basics," page 20, for tool requirements and sawing techniques.)

This feeder needs to be mounted on a deck railing, a post, or a pipe. This version specifies pipe mounting. (See "Building Basics," page 23, for mounting techniques.)

The Country Store Feeder is built principally from ACX (exterior) ⅜-inch plywood. A piece approximately 2 by 3 feet should be more than necessary for all the required pieces. Several small pieces of soft pine, preferably planed or resawn to ½ inch and ⁵⁄₁₆ inch, are required for the trim (see discussion of materials in "Building Basics," page 24).

Simple to construct and if mounted on a nearby deck railing, the Country Store Feeder will attract a wide variety of birds.

Building Steps

1. You will begin this feeder project by sawing pieces from the ⅜-inch plywood. Use hand tools or a table or radial arm saw, if available. Install a blade designed for cutting plywood or a smooth-cut cabinet blade. Cut the roof and base according to the specifications in the Materials List. Also saw the sides, back, front, and dispenser board. All these are square-cuts.

2. To saw the window cutouts in the plywood front, you will need to use a jigsaw, coping saw, or scroll saw. Draw the cutout on the piece according to the illustration. Drill a saw-access hole inside each window opening, using a ¼-inch bit. Then saw the openings. Smooth the inside edges with a rasp or sandpaper. Take care with the rasp so that you don't damage the outside veneer of the plywood.

3. Now back to the table saw to cut the window and side trim. Because these are such thin pieces, the safest way to make them is to rip the strips off pieces of pine that have already been sized to the proper thickness—in this case, ½ inch and ⁵⁄₁₆ inch. This can be done by resawing or planing down several pieces of standard ¾-inch-thick pine. If you do the resawing yourself, use a band saw or table saw. Use a push stick and a feather-board hold-down. Take care; your fingers get very close to the saw.

4. Saw the two ¾-inch square front posts from the pine stock.

5. In this step you will cut the clear plastic for the windows. The plastic can be sawn, so long as a fine-cut

Materials List

The Country Store Feeder is built principally from ACX (exterior) ⅜-inch plywood. A piece approximately 2 by 3 feet should be more than necessary for all the required pieces. Several small pieces of soft pine, preferably planed or resawn to ½ inch and ⁵⁄₁₆ inch, are required for the trim. (See "Building Basics," page 24, for discussion of materials.)

Lumber

Piece	No. of Pieces	Thickness	Width	Length
Roof	1	⅜" plywood	13"	13"
Bottom or floor	1	⅜" plywood	4⅜"	5½"
Sides	2	⅜" plywood	5½"	6"
Back	1	⅜" plywood	6"	11"
Front	1	⅜" plywood	5½"	11"
Dispenser board	1	⅜" plywood	8¼"	10⅜"
Window trim	6	⅛"	⁵⁄₁₆"	4"
Side trim	11	⅛"	½"	6"
Front post	2	¾"	¾"	5¼"

Hardware and Miscellaneous

Item	Quantity	Size	Description
⅛" clear plastic	2	2⅝" × 3½"	For the front window
Finishing nails	40	¾"	Galvanized or aluminum
Brads	50	½"	Finishing, with no heads
Glue	1 small can		Waterproof
Glue	1 stick		Hot-melt
Wood filler	¼ pint		
Sandpaper		80–120 grit	Medium
Finish	1 pint		Exterior primer and paint
Hinges	1	1" × 1"	Brass, with screws
Hooks and eyes	2	⅛" × ¾"	Brass or plated
Screws	6	1" × #6 or #8	Brass or galvanized, flat head
Iron pipe	1	½" × 6'	Galvanized, threaded one end
Floor flange	1	½" female	Galvanized

blade is used. Feed the plastic pieces slowly, and hold them firmly down on the table to prevent chattering.

6. Set the pieces together on your workbench. Check for fit and refer to the illustration (page 100) to ensure correct placement. If everything is all right, give all the pieces a thorough sanding to remove the saw marks, "fuzz," splinters, and the like and to smooth the surfaces. Fill any edge voids with wood filler. Let it dry and then sand it flush with the surface.

7. Use the waterproof glue and the nails to join the sides, front, and back. Then glue and nail the floor into position. Let the glue dry thoroughly.

8. As shown in the illustration, insert the dispenser board at an angle, inside the feeder. Use the hot-melt glue to hold it in place. If desired, drive in a few nails for additional strength.

9. Attach the side trim pieces to the 4 corners of the feeder, using the waterproof glue and brads. Do the same in the front to form the door opening. Nail the window trim into place around the window openings. See the illustration for the correct trim locations.

10. Hold one of the clear plastic windows against the inside of the front openings. Glue it into place with the hot-melt glue.

11. Drill pilot holes for the 1-inch screws in the front corners of the base. Countersink the holes on the bottom. To attach the square posts,

drive screws through the ¾-inch square posts and into the pilot holes. You might want to drill a pilot hole in the ends of the posts to reduce the chance of splitting. Note that the posts are attached only at the bottom—not to the roof.

12. You may want to add a low ledge, or railing, to help hold the seed on the feeding platform. If so, saw the railing from the ¾-inch pine or use some scraps of molding found around your shop. (Choose quarter-round molding or any other style that strikes your fancy.) Then cut the molding to length and glue or tack it into place.

13. You will attach the roof by using 1-inch hinges. Using screws, fasten the hinge into the back edge of the roof; do the same to the back piece. Check the illustration for correct location.

14. If the feeder is to be post-mounted, screw and glue a mounting spacer block to the bottom of the base (see the section on mounting in "Building Basics," page 23). If a pipe mount is used, the floor flange can be screwed on after the finishing step.

15. Give the feeder a final sanding. To help mask the strong plywood grain, use a primer paint on the outside before applying exterior paint. Use subdued colors; some birds don't like the bright ones. A second color on the trim will help make the feeder attractive.

16. If the feeder is to be pipe-mounted, screw the floor flange onto the set pipe. Add seed and you are ready for the birds.

Country Store Feeder

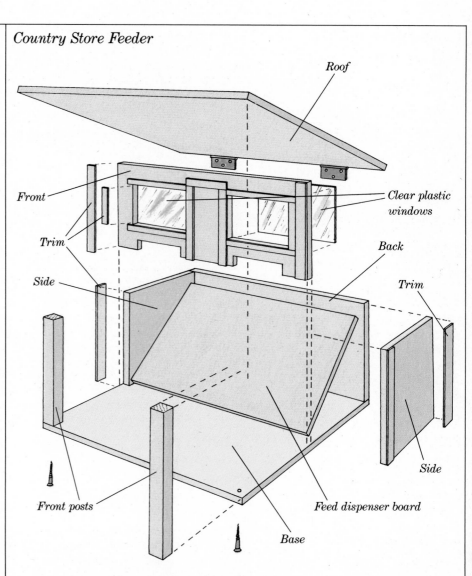

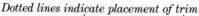

Dotted lines indicate placement of trim

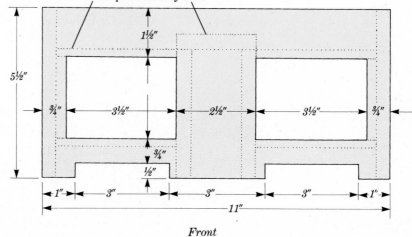

Front

MULTISEED FEEDER

*T**his bird feeder will quickly let you know the favorite foods of your feathered visitors. Four different types of birdseed can be dispensed simultaneously from each of the four dispensers. The windows let you know when it's time for a refill.*

Description and Tool Requirements

This project calls for a table or radial arm saw to cut the square pieces as well as make the necessary kerf slots and dadoes. A jigsaw or band saw is needed to make the curved cuts. A hot-melt glue gun would be useful. In addition, you need several bar or pipe clamps. (Refer to "Building Basics," page 20, for tool requirements and sawing techniques.)

This feeder can be mounted on a deck railing, a post, or a pipe stand (the version presented specifies pipe-stand mounting). It can also be hung by attaching the wires to the outside of the feeder base. (See "Building Basics," page 23, for mounting techniques and parts requirements.)

Building Steps

1. While you still have the 6-feet length of 1 by 12, use a table saw to cut the edging strip. Pick the best edge of the board and the one with the straightest grain. If need be, joint or edge-saw the piece to get a clean edge. Using a fine-cut carbide or steel cabinet saw, rip off a strip a little less than ⅛ inch thick and about

Experiment with four different kinds of birdseed at a time to see which variety the birds prefer.

54 inches long. Test the strength of the strip by bending it in a circle.

2. Saw 3 pieces off the 1 by 12 to make the roof and base. Rip one piece down the middle. Using your pipe or bar clamps, edge-glue the wide pieces to the narrow pieces to make 2 boards about 16¾ inches wide; be sure to use the waterproof glue. As you clamp, carefully align the edges so they are flush.

3. While the glue is drying, get out your jigsaw or band saw. Using a compass (or a pencil tied to a string anchored by a tack), lay out a 16-inch-diameter circle on one of the pieces. Temporarily join the 2 pieces for gang-sawing. (See "Building Basics," page 21, on duplicate cutting for more details.) Saw the circles carefully, staying as close to the line as possible. While the 2 circles are still joined, smooth the edges by sanding. Then separate the pieces.

4. Go back to the table saw to cut the roof blocks, center supports, corner supports, and end corner supports from the cedar lumber. There are 4 of each of these pieces.

5. To cut the clear plastic windows, use a table saw with a fine-tooth blade. Feed the plastic pieces slowly, and hold them firmly down on the table to prevent chattering.

6. Install your thickest saw blade; a blade with a kerf of ⅛ inch or greater works best. Saw the kerf slots, ¼ inch deep, in all the support pieces (see the illustration on page 103). Both edges of the center supports should be grooved; on the corner supports, one edge of each should be grooved. Check to see if the clear plastic window material slides easily into the slots. If not, make a second pass, shifting the fence over ever so slightly, to enlarge the groove.

7. Mount a ¼-inch dado blade on your table saw. Cut the ¼-inch grooves, ⅜ inch deep, down the center of the center supports. If you don't have a ¼-inch dado blade, cut this groove by making multiple passes.

Materials List

The Multiseed Feeder is built from surfaced 1 by 12 western red cedar and ¼-inch ACX (exterior) plywood. Redwood or pine can also be used. A board 6 feet long should easily do the job. The piece should be relatively free of knots and defects. Less than 1 square foot of plywood is needed. (See "Building Basics," page 24, for discussion of materials.)

Lumber

Piece	No. of Pieces	Thickness	Width	Length
Strip edging	1	⅛"	¾"	54"
Roof and base	3	¾"	11⅛"	16½"
Roof blocks	4	¾"	4¾"	4¾"
Center supports	4	¾"	2½"	5"
Corner supports	4	¾"	1¼"	5"
End corner supports	4	¾"	½"	5"
Separators	2	¼" plywood	5"	10⅝"

Hardware and Miscellaneous

Item	Quantity	Size	Description
⅛" clear plastic	2	3" × 4¼"	For the windows
Finishing nails	20	¾"	Headed, galvanized or aluminum
Finishing nails	40	1½"	Galvanized or aluminum
Glue	1 small can		Waterproof
Glue	1 or 2 sticks		Hot melt
Sandpaper		80–120 grit	Medium
Finish	1 pint		Exterior primer and paint
Screws	6	1" × #6 or #8	Brass or galvanized, flat head
Iron pipe	1	½" × 6'	Galvanized, threaded one end
Floor flange	1	½" female	Galvanized

8. Now saw the two ¼-inch plywood separators. A ¼-inch slot, 1½ inches deep, needs to be sawn in the center of each piece. Although this can be done on your table saw, it is safer to saw these slots by using your jigsaw or band saw. Temporarily join the 2 pieces together for gang-sawing. Draw the slot on the top piece and carefully saw around the outline.

9. Check the pieces for fit. Refer to the illustration to double-check placement. After making any necessary corrections, give all the pieces a sanding to remove the saw marks, "fuzz," and splinters and to smooth the surfaces. Fill any edge voids in the plywood with wood filler. Let the filler dry and then sand it flush.

10. Start the assembly by joining the 2 plywood separators into a cross, sliding one slot into the other. Use the hot-melt glue to seal the center. Using a framing square, check to make sure the 2 pieces are perpendicular to each other. Make any necessary adjustments.

11. Using the waterproof glue, glue and insert the ¼-inch plywood separator into the ¼-inch grooves in the center supports. Align the edges so they are flush; clamp the glued pieces together.

12. When the glue is dry, you will attach the assembly you made in step 11 to the center of the base. To do

this, trace the outline of the separator assembly on the bottom of the base. Then turn the base over, place it on top of the assembly, and carefully drive finishing nails up through the bottom. You may find it helpful to use a few drops of the hot-melt glue to hold the pieces in place while nailing up through the bottom.

13. Fabricate the 4 corner assemblies. With the waterproof glue fasten the end corner pieces so they are flush against the side of the corner pieces. Nail the pieces together.

14. Now, using the same techniques as in step 12, position, glue, and nail the corner assemblies to the base. Insert the plastic windows into the kerf slots. Use the hot-melt glue to fix the windows in place. Allow at least a ⅝-inch to ¾-inch space at the bottom so the seed can flow freely (see the illustration for details).

15. After all glue is dry, you will attach the edging strip to the circular edge of the base. Apply the waterproof glue, then carefully nail the strip into place with ¾-inch finishing nails. Cut off any extra stripping where the ends meet. Note: If the strip resists bending, soak it in warm water for a while.

16. Check the illustration to learn the positions of the roof blocks, which will help keep the circular roof in place when the wind blows. Attach the blocks, using the waterproof glue and finishing nails. When the roof is in place, there should be a ¼-inch gap between the blocks and the crossed separators.

17. If the feeder is to be post-mounted, use the waterproof glue and screws to fasten a mounting spacer block to the bottom of the base (see the section on mounting in

"Building Basics," page 23). If a pipe mount is used, the floor flange can be screwed on after applying finish.

18. Give the feeder a final sanding. If you used cedar or redwood in the construction, an oil stain will provide weather protection and look attractive. If you used pine, paint the outside of the Multiseed Feeder. Use a dull color.

19. If the feeder is to be pipe-mounted, screw the floor flange on to the set pipe, add seed, and you are ready for the birds.

Multiseed Feeder

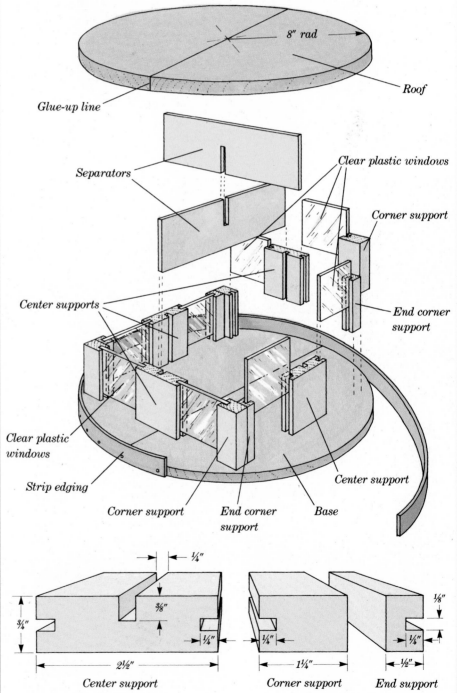

8" rad

Roof

Glue-up line

Separators

Clear plastic windows

Corner support

End corner support

Center supports

Clear plastic windows

Strip edging

Corner support

End corner support

Base

Center support

¼"

⅜"

¾"

¼"

2½"

Center support

¼"

1¼"

Corner support

⅛"

¼"

½"

End support

QUICK-MARKET FEEDER

This convenience store look-alike is bound to have a lot of customers, because it has a divider in the center that allows you to serve two different kinds of birdseed. There is no ledge on this feeder; this is to allow seed to fall off to be eaten by the birds that are primarily ground feeders.

Description and Tool Requirements

This project calls for a table saw or radial arm saw to cut the square, straight-edged pieces and to make the angled cuts with the accuracy to ensure a tight fit. A jigsaw or band saw is needed to make the window cutouts. To cut the plastic, you need a circle saw or band saw. A hot-melt glue gun would be useful. (See "Building Basics," page 20, for tool requirements and different sawing techniques.)

This feeder can be mounted on a deck railing, a post, or a pipe. This version specifies a pipe stand. It may be possible to hang the platform by attaching the wires to the outside of the feeder and adding an extension on the back corner. (See "Building Basics," page 23, for mounting methods and parts requirements.)

Building Steps

1. Start this feeder project by cutting the base, an 11¼-inch square, out of the 1 by 12. Use a radial arm saw or table saw.

2. Now cut the two back pieces. Both have a 15-degree bevel on the top edge (see the illustration on page 105). Also cut the feeder fronts with the same bevel on the top edge. Note that both the backs and fronts come in two varieties: left and right. Each back and front piece is a different length.

The absence of a ledge on this feeder allows plenty of birdseed to fall to the ground for ground-feeding birds.

Quick-Market Feeder

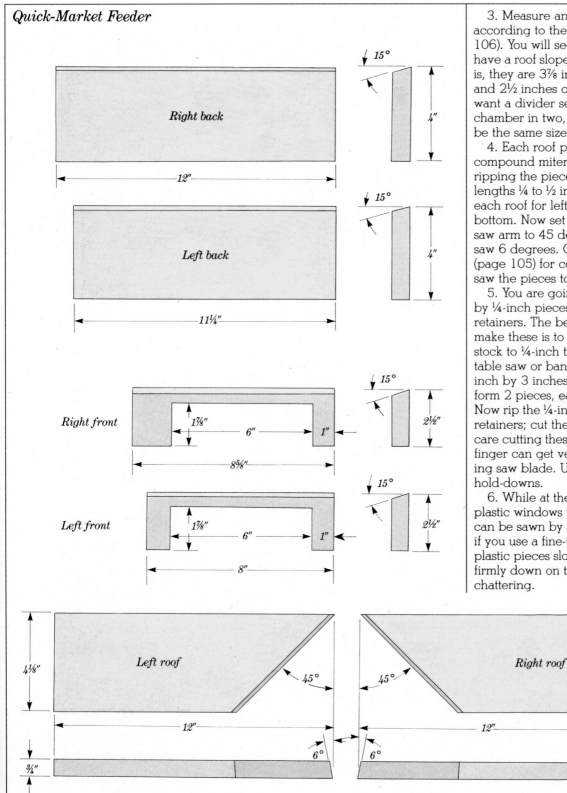

3. Measure and cut the side pieces according to the illustration (page 106). You will see that these pieces have a roof slope of 15 degrees—that is, they are 3⅞ inches on one edge, and 2½ inches on the other. If you want a divider separating the feed chamber in two, saw it now. It should be the same size as the sides.

4. Each roof piece should have a compound miter at one end. After ripping the pieces to width, cut the lengths ¼ to ½ inch overlength. Mark each roof for left or right, top or bottom. Now set your miter gauge or saw arm to 45 degrees, and tilt the saw 6 degrees. Check the illustration (page 105) for correct position, and saw the pieces to final length.

5. You are going to need some ¼-by ¼-inch pieces to serve as window retainers. The best and safest way to make these is to resaw some ¾-inch stock to ¼-inch thickness. Using a table saw or band saw, rip a piece ¾ inch by 3 inches, 7 inches long, to form 2 pieces, each ¼ inch thick. Now rip the ¼-inch-wide strips for the retainers; cut them to length. Take care cutting these small pieces—your finger can get very close to the moving saw blade. Use a push stick and hold-downs.

6. While at the saw, cut the clear plastic windows to size. The plastic can be sawn by a circle or band saw if you use a fine-tooth blade. Feed the plastic pieces slowly, and hold them firmly down on the table to prevent chattering.

Quick-Market Feeder

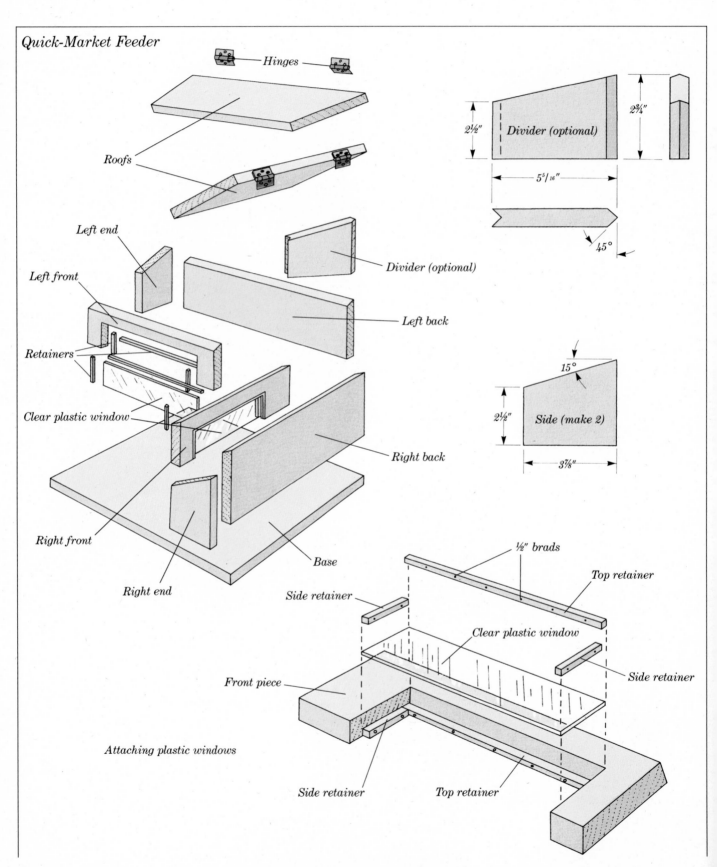

Hinges

Roofs

Divider (optional)

2½"

2¾"

5⁵/₁₆"

45°

Left end

Left front

Divider (optional)

Left back

Retainers

Clear plastic window

15°

2½"

Side (make 2)

3⅞"

Right back

Right front

Base

Right end

½" brads

Top retainer

Side retainer

Clear plastic window

Side retainer

Front piece

Attaching plastic windows

Side retainer

Top retainer

7. Now, retrieve the two front pieces. The best tool for cutting the window openings is a jigsaw or band saw. If neither is available, a hand coping saw can be used. Refer to the illustration (page 105) for the dimensions and locations of these openings. Be sure to cut the openings on the bottom, or square-edged, sides.

8. Set the pieces together on your workbench. Check the fit and use the illustration (page 106) to ensure correct placement. Mark their positions on the pieces if needed. When all is correct, give all the pieces a thorough sanding to remove the saw marks, "fuzz," splinters, and the like and to smooth the surfaces. Fill any knotholes or defects with wood filler. Let it dry and sand it flush.

9. You will start the assembly by attaching the plastic windows according to the illustration (page 106). The easiest method is to first tack the retainer strips and windows in place with small drops of hot-melt glue. Then secure them by driving brads through the retainer strips into the edges of the front-piece window cutouts. Allow at least a ½-inch opening at the bottom of the windows so the seed can flow.

10. Continue the assembly by attaching the backs and sides to the base, using 1½-inch nails and the waterproof glue. If you desire, countersink the nails and fill the holes with wood filler. When the filler dries, sand it flush. Glue and nail the long front piece flush with the butt end of the short front piece. Place the front assembly in position and attach it to the sides and base. If desired, add the divider block.

Materials List

This multiseed feeder is built from surfaced 1 by 12 western red cedar. Redwood or pine can also be used. A board 5 feet long should easily do the job. The lumber should be relatively free of knots and other imperfections. All the parts should be cut from defect-free sections. (See "Building Basics," page 24, for discussion of materials.)

Lumber

Piece	No. of Pieces	Thickness	Width	Length
Base	1	¾"	11¼"	11¼"
Back, left	1	¾"	4"	11¼"
Back, right	1	¾"	4"	12"
Front, left	1	¾"	2½"	8"
Front, right	1	¾"	2½"	8⅝"
Sides	2	¾"	2½"	3⅞"
Divider (optional)	1	¾"	2½"	3⅞"
Roofs	2	¾"	4⅛"	12"
Window retainers (top)	4	¼"	¼"	6"
Window retainers (side)	8	¼"	¼"	1¼"

Hardware and Miscellaneous

Item	Quantity	Size	Description
⅛" clear plastic	2	1½" × 6"	For the windows
Brads	24	½"	Headless
Finishing nails	24	1½"	Galvanized or aluminum
Glue	1 small can		Waterproof
Glue	1 or 2 sticks		Hot melt
Sandpaper		80–120 grit	Medium
Finish	1 pint		Exterior oil stain
Hinges	2	¾" × 1"	Brass, with screws
Screws	4	¾" × #8	Brass, flat head
Iron pipe	1	½" × 6'	Galvanized, threaded one end
Floor flange	1	½" female	Galvanized

11. The roof pieces will be hinged to the back, as shown in the illustration (page 106). Use 2 hinges per roof piece, attaching the hinges by driving screws into the back edge of the roofs and the backs.

12. Give the feeder a final sanding: round edges, sand away glue smear, and the like. If cedar or redwood was used, the feeder can be left unfinished and it will weather to an attractive gray. If you want to weatherproof the feeder, finish the outside with exterior oil stain. If you used pine, exterior enamel paint is the preferred finish.

13. If the feeder is to be mounted on a pipe stand, attach a floor flange onto the center of the base by using the four ¾-inch screws. After the pipe has been set in the ground, screw the flange onto it. Add seeds and prepare to serve hungry patrons.

TWO-STORY FEEDER

***W**ith a two-story bird feeder you may be able to increase the bird traffic in your backyard. This unique two-story feeder provides plenty of room for the larger birds on the top level and for smaller ones on the bottom level.*

Description and Tool Requirements

Building this interesting feeder requires a table saw in addition to basic hand tools. A jigsaw, coping saw, or scroll saw are needed to cut the inside circles. A drill with ⁵/₃₂-, ¼-, and 1-inch bits are required to make the various holes.

The slats for the center barrel are thin. Step 2 describes how to plane ¾-inch material to ½-inch material. If you don't have a planer, a local lumberyard or cabinet shop may plane the slats for you.

The feeder must be mounted on a post or pipe. (See "Building Basics," page 23, for mounting techniques.)

Building Steps

1. While you still have a long length of 1 by 8, you will saw the 44-inch edging strips. Move to the table saw and install your smoothest-cutting blade. Now, select a clean, unmarred edge of the 1 by 8; it should have straight grain. (Rip the edge smooth if necessary.) Rip two ⅛-inch strips from the board. Recheck to make sure the grain is straight.

2. For the barrel slats, or sides, you are going to need a number of pieces ¼-inch thick by ½-inch wide. Sawing and resawing these pieces between the fence and saw on the table saw can be laborious and dangerous. It will be much easier if you start with ½-inch stock, then rip off ¼-inch-wide strips, using a push stick and a hold-down board.

The obvious way to cut the ½-inch material is to plane a ¾-inch piece down to ½-inch thick (you need only about 3 feet of 8-inch-wide lumber).

If a planer is not available, see if your lumberyard has ½-inch material in stock or can plane a piece for you. Most neighborhood cabinet shops will custom plane if asked.

Another approach is to resaw (split) the ¾-inch stock on the band saw, and plane it to ¼-inch thickness. Then saw ½-inch strips off the board for the slats.

However you make the slats, remember that sawing thin strips can be dangerous. Use push sticks and hold-downs (see "Building Basics,"

The two feeding platforms encourage birds of various sizes to feed simultaneously.

page 20, for discussion of sawing thin material). Saw a couple of extra slats.

3. You will use a table saw to cut the rest of the pieces. From the 1 by 8, cut the square blanks for the inside top and center divider; both blanks are 6½ inches square. From the ⅜-inch plywood, cut the 15-inch square blanks for the feeder tables, bottom, and lid. If you are going to mount the feeder on a wood post, cut the mounting boards and spacer block.

4. Next, you will gang-saw the circles for the feeder tables. Temporarily join the 2 squares of 15-inch plywood (see "Building Basics," page 21, for techniques of duplicate cutting). On the top square draw the 14-inch-diameter circle by using a large compass or a pencil tied to a string anchored by a tack. Then draw the 6¾-inch hole. The outside circle can be cut with either a band saw or a jigsaw. The jigsaw must be used for sawing the inside circle. Use a ¼-inch or ½-inch bit to drill a saw-access hole, then carefully saw the inside hole. A coping saw or scroll saw can also be used for this cut.

Sand both the inside and outside edges while the pieces are still joined. A disk or belt sander would work well on the outside, a drum sander on the inside. Use a rasp or sanding block if these sanders are not available. Separate the pieces after they have been sanded.

5. Draw a 7-inch circle on the plywood lid blank; cut the circle. Draw an 8-inch circle on the 9-inch square bottom; cut the circle. Sand the edges of both circles.

6. For gang-sawing, temporarily join the square inside top and the center divider. With a jigsaw or band saw, carefully draw and cut a 6¼-inch circle. Note: Saw the circle slightly oversize; the center divider must fit securely inside the feeder barrel. Lightly sand the edges and separate the two pieces. After the

Materials List

This feeder would look especially attractive if built with western red cedar and finished with an oil stain. Other textured softwoods such as pine can, of course, be used. You will need a piece of 1 by 8 approximately 5 feet long. The lumber should be straight grained, of good grade, and relatively free of large knots or other defects. A short block of 2 by 4 is needed for mounting. (See "Building Basics," page 24, for discussion of materials.) A 2' × 3' piece of ⅜" ACX (exterior) sanded plywood is also needed.

Lumber

Piece	No. of Pieces	Thickness	Width	Length
Edging, or rim strips	2	⅛"	¾"	44"
Slats, or sides	37	¼"	½"	10½"
Inside top blank	1	¾"	6½"	6½"
Center divider blank	1	¾"	6½"	6½"
Mounting boards*	2	¾"	3½"	6"
Mounting spacer block*	1	1½"	3½"	3½"
Mounting post*	1	3½"	3½"	5–7'
Feeder table blanks	2	⅜"	15"	15"
Bottom blank	1	⅜"	9"	9"
Lid blank	1	⅜"	8"	8"

* If post-mounted

Hardware and Miscellaneous

Item	Quantity	Size	Description
Brads	100 (approx.)	¾"	Headed
Finishing nails	20	1"–1¼"	
Wood filler	1 tube		
Glue			Waterproof
Sandpaper	1 sheet	80–120 grit	Medium
Finish	1 pint		Exterior oil stain
Iron Pipe**	1	½" × 5–7'	Galvanized, threaded
Floor flange**	1	½" female	Galvanized
Screws*	2	1¼" × #8	Brass, flat head
Screws**	4	¾" × #8	Brass or galvanized, flat head

* If post-mounted
** If pipe-mounted

barrel is constructed, the divider can be further sanded for a snug fit.

7. The center divider has two tangents sawn for feed shoots (see the illustration on page 110 for details). These tangents are 1-inch deep and 4½-inches wide, directly across from each other. Saw them by using your jigsaw or band saw. Sand smooth.

8. Now give all the parts a light sanding to remove "fuzz" and slightly round the edges.

9. You are now ready to start assembly. Put the lower feeder table on its edge in a padded vise. Using ¾-inch brads and glue, tack 4 or 5 slats

flush with the edge of the table, on the inside circle. Now remove the assembly from the vise, insert the upper feeder table 5 inches from the bottom table, and glue and tack the slats in place. Make certain they are tight against each other. Continue to glue and tack more strips. Measure the distance between the two tables frequently; it should always be 5 inches and the assembly should be square.

Tack all the slats into the circle. The final slat may need to be ripped down for a tight fit.

10. If you plan on mounting the feeder on a wood post, attach the mounting divider block, apply the waterproof glue, center the block on the bottom piece, and drive the 1¼-inch screws through the bottom into the 2 by 4 block. Note: This mount is designed for a 4 by 4 post. If some other size is used, the spacer block size needs to be adjusted. Ignore this step if a pipe mount is intended.

11. Fit the bottom into the barrel. If the fit is too tight, sand or rasp the bottom for a snug fit. Glue the bottom in place (hot-melt glue works well for this purpose). Then nail the bottom into place, using 1-inch finishing nails. Drive the nails at an angle. If needed, use a countersink to help home the angled nails.

12. Now fit the center divider into the barrel. If it is too tight, sand again for a snug fit. Slide the divider down the feeder until it is at the same level as the upper feeder table. Glue and nail the divider into place. Again, hot-melt glue can be used.

13. Fit the inner top into the barrel; it should be a fairly loose fit. If needed, lightly saw or sand to accomplish this. Center the inner top on the plywood lid, then attach the pieces, using glue and nails.

14. In this step you will drill the 1-inch feed holes for the 2 levels. Drill the 2 upper feed holes immediately above the upper feeding table at 90 degrees from the tangent feed shoots in the center divider. Drill the 2 lower feed holes 90 degrees from the upper ones, just below the feed shoots. They should be immediately adjacent to the lower feeder table (refer to the illustration for help in placing these holes).

15. Finally, fit the edging or rim strips, trimming as necessary, then glue and nail them around the circumference of the two feeder tables. (Again, look carefully at the illustration for details.)

16. With wood filler, fill any voids in the visible plywood edges. When the filler is dry, sand smooth. Give the entire feeder a last sanding. If cedar was used, apply an oil stain to the outside to enhance appearance and weather resistance. Painting with an exterior paint is the other alternative. Use a muted paint because some birds don't like bright colors.

17. Mount the feeder. Refer to the discussion on mounting in ''Building Basics,'' on page 23.

Two-Story Feeder

Lid — 7"

Inside lid — 6¼"

14"

Slats

Center divider

6¼"

10½"

6¾"

Feed shoot
1" × 4½"

Edging

Feeder tables

8"

Bottom

INDEX

Note: Page numbers in boldface type indicate principal references; page numbers in italic type indicate references to illustrations.

A

Alpine Bird Feeder, *80*, **80–83**
American Kestrel Home, *63*, **63–65**

B

Band saw, techniques with, 21, 25
Barky wood, 24
Baths. *See* Birdbaths
Bench scroll saw, techniques with, 21
Berries, 6
Birdbaths, 7, 8, *8*
Birdhouses, 27–65
  American Kestrel Home, *63*, **63–65**
  Bluebird Tree House, 24, **44–45**, *45*
  Chickadee Condominium, *60*, **60–62**
  cleaning, 14, 15, *15*
  finishing, 23
  Flycatcher Chalet, *31*, **31–33**
  House Finch Country Home, *28*, **28–30**
  materials for, 15, 22, 24–25
  mounting, 23, *23*
  placement of, 15
  Purple Martin Condo, *53*, **53–59**
  requirements for, 13–14
  Robin's Roost, *38*, **38–39**
  Screech-Owl Box, 24, *46*, **46–47**
  Tree Swallow House, *34*, **34–37**
  Wood Duck Nesting Box, *26–27*
  Woodpecker Homestead, *48*, **48–49**
  Wren Apartment House, *40*, **40–43**
Blackbird, Red-winged, feeding, 10 (chart)
Bluebirds
  Bluebird Tree House, 24, **44–45**, *45*
  feeding, 10 (chart)
  Flycatcher Chalet for, 31
  nesting, *13*

Blue Jays
  feeding, 10 (chart)
  habitat for, 7
Buntings, feeding, 10 (chart)
Buying wood, 24–25

C

Carousel Feeder, *76*, **76–79**
Catbird, Gray, feeding, 10 (chart)
Cats, providing cover from, 7, 8
Cedar
  advantages of, 24
  leaving unfinished, 23
Chat, Yellow-breasted, feeding, 10 (chart)
Chickadees, 60
  Chickadee Condominium, *60*, **60–62**
  feeding, 10 (chart)
Circular saw, *19*, 21
Clamps, 20
Coping saw, techniques with, 21
Country Gazebo Feeder, *92*, **92–97**
Country Store Feeder, *98*, **98–100**
Cowbird, Brown-headed, feeding, 10 (chart)
Crossbills
  habitat for, 6
  Red, feeding, 10 (chart)
Crow, American, feeding, 10 (chart)

D

Doves
  as ground feeders, 12
  Mourning, feeding, 10 (chart)
Drill press, 20, 22

E, F

Evergreens, 6, 7
Falcons, American Kestrel Home, *63*, **63–65**
Feeders, 67–110
  Alpine, *80*, **80–83**
  Carousel, *76*, **76–79**
  Country Gazebo, *92*, **92–97**
  Country Store, *98*, **98–100**
  Hummingbird, *72*, **72–73**
  Lighthouse, *66–67*, *68*, **68–71**
  Multiseed, *101*, **101–3**
  placement of, 7, 12
  Quick-Market, *104*, **104–7**
  Suet, *74*, **74–75**
  Two-Story, *108*, **108–10**

Feeders (*continued*)
  Weather Vane, *88*, **88–91**
  Window Coaxing, *84*, **84–87**
Feeding, 9, 10–11 (chart), 12
Finches
  feeding, 10 (chart)
  habitat for, 6
  House Finch Country Home, *28*, **28–30**
Finishing, 23
Fir, true, 24
Flicker, Northern, nesting, *14*
Flycatcher Chalet, *31*, **31–33**

G

Glues, 25
Goldfinches, feeding, 10 (chart)
Grackles, feeding, 10 (chart)
Grains, 7
Grasses, 6, 7
Grosbeaks, feeding, 10 (chart)
Ground-Doves, feeding, 10 (chart)
Ground-feeding birds
  Quick-Market Feeder for, 104
  spills eaten by, 12
Grouse, Ruffed, feeding, 10 (chart)

H

Habitats, creating, 6–8
Handsaws, *20*, 21
Hardware, 25
Hawks, protection from, 12
Holes, drilling, 22
House Finch Country Home, *28*, **28–30**
Hummingbird Feeder, *72*, **72–73**

J, K

Jays
  feeding, 10 (chart)
  habitat for, 7
Jigsaw, techniques with, 21
Juncos, feeding, 10 (chart)
Kerfing plywood, 22
Kestrels, American Kestrel Home, *63*, **63–65**
Kinglet, Ruby-crowned, feeding, 10 (chart)

L

Lark, Horned, feeding, 10 (chart)
Lighthouse Bird Feeder, *66–67*, *68*, **68–71**

Longspur, Lapland, feeding, 10 (chart)
Lumber
  choosing, 15, 24
  sizes of, 24–25

M, N

Martin, Purple
  feeding, 10 (chart)
  habitat for, 53
  Purple Martin Condo, *53*, **53–59**
Materials, 15, 22, 24–25
Meadowlarks, feeding, 10 (chart)
Mice, discouraging, 15
Mites, preventing, 15
Mockingbirds, feeding, 10 (chart)
Molding, buying, 24–25
Mounting a birdhouse, 23, *23*
Multiseed Feeder, *101*, **101–3**
Nails, 25
Native plants, 6
Nesting material, providing, 13, *13*, 14
Nuthatches, feeding, 10 (chart)

O, P

Orioles, feeding, 10 (chart)
Owl, Screech-Owl Box, 24, *46*, **46–47**
Patterns, using, 21–22
Pheasants, feeding, 10 (chart)
Pigeon, Band-tailed, feeding, 11 (chart)
Pine, 24
Planer, techniques with, 25
Plants, 6–7
Plywood
  choosing, 22, 24
  kerfing, 22
Power tools
  drill press, 20, 22
  sanders, 22
  saws, 18, *18–19*, 20, 22
Predatory birds, protection from, 12
Purple Martin. *See* Martin, Purple
Pyracantha, 6
Pyrrhuloxia, feeding, 11 (chart)

Q, R

Quails, feeding, 11 (chart)
Quick-Market Feeder, *104*, **104–7**

Radial arm saw, *18*
techniques with, 20, 22
Reciprocating saw, *19*
Redwood
advantages of, 24
leaving unfinished, 23
Resawing wood, 25
Robin, American, *4–5*
feeding, 11 (chart)
Robin's Roost, *38,* **38–39**

S

Saber saw, *19,* 21
Sanders, power, *19*
Sanding, 22
Sapsucker, Yellow-bellied, feeding, 11 (chart)
Saws
hand, *20,* 21
power, 18, *18–19,* 20, 22
techniques with, 20–22, *21*
Screech-Owl Box, 24, *46,* **46–47**
Screws, 25
Scroll saw, 20
Seed-eating birds, habitat for, 7
Shrikes, protection from, 12
Shrubs, placement of, 7
Siskin, Pine, feeding, 11 (chart)
Slabwood, buying, 24
Sparrows
feeding, 11 (chart)
as ground feeders, 12
House, discouraging, 15
Spruce, 24
Squirrels, discouraging, 15
Starlings
discouraging, 15
feeding, 11 (chart)
Suet Feeder, *74,* **74–75**
Summer feeding, 12
Swallows, Tree
Flycatcher Chalet for, 31
Tree Swallow House, *34,* **34–37**

T

Table saw, *18,* 20
kerfing plywood with, 22
resawing wood with, 25
straight cuts with, 20
Tanagers, feeding, 11 (chart)
Techniques
curved cuts, 21
drilling holes, 22
Techniques (*continued*)
duplicate cuts, 21–22
finishing a birdhouse, 23
kerfing plywood, 22
mounting a birdhouse, 23, *23*
resawing wood, 25
sanding, 22
straight cuts, 20–21
transferring shapes from illustrations, 22
Thrashers, feeding, 11 (chart)
Thrushes, feeding, 11 (chart)
Titmouse, Tufted, feeding, 11 (chart)
Tools, *16–17*
power, 18, *18–19,* 20, 22
Towhees, feeding, 11 (chart)
Tree Swallows
Flycatcher Chalet for, 31
Tree Swallow House, *34,* **34–37**
Two-Story Feeder, *108,* **108–10**

V, W

Variety, importance of, 6, 7
Vises, 20
Warblers, feeding, 11 (chart)
Water, providing, 7–8
Waxwing, Cedar, feeding, 11 (chart)
Weather Vane Feeder, *88,* **88–91**
Window Coaxing Feeder, *84,* **84–87**
Wind protection, Weather Vane Feeder for, 88
Winter feeding, 9, 10–11 (chart), 12
Winter shelter, birdhouses for, 15
Wood Duck Nesting Box, *50,* **50–52**
Woodpeckers
Downy, Flycatcher Chalet for, 31
feeding, 11 (chart)
habitat for, 7
Red-bellied, 11 (chart), 48
Woodpecker Homestead, *48,* **48–49**
Wrens
feeding, 11 (chart)
swaying house tolerated by, 14
Wren Apartment House, *40,* **40–43**

U.S./Metric Measure Conversion Chart

	Symbol	*Formulas for Exact Measures* When you know:	Multiply by:	To find:	*Rounded Measures for Quick Reference*		
Mass (Weight)	oz	ounces	28.35	grams	1 oz		= 30 g
	lb	pounds	0.45	kilograms	4 oz		= 115 g
	g	grams	0.035	ounces	8 oz		= 225 g
	kg	kilograms	2.2	pounds	16 oz	= 1 lb	= 450 g
					32 oz	= 2 lb	= 900 g
					36 oz	= 2¼ lb	= 1000 g (1 kg)
Volume	tsp	teaspoons	5.0	milliliters	¼ tsp	= 1/24 oz	= 1 ml
	tbsp	tablespoons	15.0	milliliters	½ tsp	= 1/12 oz	= 2 ml
	fl oz	fluid ounces	29.57	milliliters	1 tsp	= ⅙ oz	= 5 ml
	c	cups	0.24	liters	1 tbsp	= ½ oz	= 15 ml
	pt	pints	0.47	liters	1 c	= 8 oz	= 250 ml
	qt	quarts	0.95	liters	2 c (1 pt)	= 16 oz	= 500 ml
	gal	gallons	3.785	liters	4 c (1 qt)	= 32 oz	= 1 liter
	ml	milliliters	0.034	fluid ounces	4 qt (1 gal)	= 128 oz	= 3¾ liter
Length	in.	inches	2.54	centimeters	⅜ in.	= 1 cm	
	ft	feet	30.48	centimeters	1 in.	= 2.5 cm	
	yd	yards	0.9144	meters	2 in.	= 5 cm	
	mi	miles	1.609	kilometers	2½ in.	= 6.5 cm	
	km	kilometers	0.621	miles	12 in. (1 ft)	= 30 cm	
	m	meters	1.094	yards	1 yd	= 90 cm	
	cm	centimeters	0.39	inches	100 ft	= 30 m	
					1 mi	= 1.6 km	
Temperature	°F	Fahrenheit	5/9 (after subtracting 32)	Celsius	32° F	= 0° C	
					68°F	= 20°C	
	°C	Celsius	9/5 (then add 32)	Fahrenheit	212° F	= 100° C	
Area	in.²	square inches	6.452	square centimeters	1 in.²	= 6.5 cm²	
	ft²	square feet	929.0	square centimeters	1 ft²	= 930 cm²	
	yd²	square yards	8361.0	square centimeters	1 yd²	= 8360 cm²	
	a.	acres	0.4047	hectares	1 a.	= 4050 m²	